Developing Web Components with TypeScript

Native Web Development Using Thin Libraries

Jörg Krause

Apress®

Developing Web Components with TypeScript: Native Web Development Using Thin Libraries

Jörg Krause
Berlin, Berlin, Germany

ISBN-13 (pbk): 978-1-4842-6839-1   ISBN-13 (electronic): 978-1-4842-6840-7
https://doi.org/10.1007/978-1-4842-6840-7

Managing Director, Apress Media LLC: Welmoed Spahr
Acquisitions Editor: Spandana Chatterjee
Development Editor: Matthew Moodie
Coordinating Editor: Shrikant Vishwakarma

Cover designed by eStudioCalamar

Cover image designed by Pexels

Distributed to the book trade worldwide by Springer Science+Business Media LLC, 1 New York Plaza, Suite 4600, New York, NY 10004. Phone 1-800-SPRINGER, fax (201) 348-4505, e-mail orders-ny@springer-sbm. com, or visit www.springeronline.com. Apress Media, LLC is a California LLC and the sole member (owner) is Springer Science + Business Media Finance Inc (SSBM Finance Inc). SSBM Finance Inc is a **Delaware** corporation.

For information on translations, please e-mail booktranslations@springernature.com; for reprint, paperback, or audio rights, please e-mail bookpermissions@springernature.com, or visit www.apress.com/ rights-permissions.

Apress titles may be purchased in bulk for academic, corporate, or promotional use. eBook versions and licenses are also available for most titles. For more information, reference our Print and eBook Bulk Sales web page at www.apress.com/bulk-sales.

Any source code or other supplementary material referenced by the author in this book is available to readers on GitHub via the book's product page, located at www.apress.com/978-1-4842-6839-1. For more detailed information, please visit www.apress.com/source-code.

Printed on acid-free paper

Writing outstanding code requires a mixture of craftsmanship, engineering, and art. To master all of this, one need a lot of time in front of a computer.

For all people around me accepting my focus.

Table of Contents

About the Author

Jörg Krause has been working with software and software technology since the early 1980s, beginning with a ZX 81 and taking his first steps as a programmer in BASIC and assembly language. He studied information technology at Humboldt University, Berlin, but left early, in the 1990s, to start his own company. He has worked with Internet technology and software development since the early days when CompuServe and FidoNet dominated. He has worked with Microsoft technologies and software since Windows 95. In 1998, he worked on one of the first commercial e-commerce solutions and wrote his first book. Due to its wide success, he started working as a freelance consultant and author in order to share his experience and knowledge with others. He has written several books for Apress, Hanser, Addison-Wesley, and other major publishers along with several self-published books for a total of over 60 titles. He also publishes articles in magazines and speaks at major conferences in Germany. Currently, Jörg works as an independent consultant, software developer, and author in Berlin, Germany.

In his occasional spare time, Jörg enjoys reading thrillers and science fiction novels and going on a round of golf.

Follow him on Twitter at `@joergisgeek` for updates and insights.

About the Technical Reviewer

Yogendra Sharma is a developer with experience in architecture, design, and development of scalable and distributed applications with a core interest in microservices and Spring. Currently he is working as an IoT and Cloud Architect at Intelizign Engineering Services Pvt Pune. He also has hands-on experience in technologies such as AWS, IoT, Python, J2SE, J2EE, NodeJS, VueJs, Angular, MongoDB, and Docker. He constantly explores technical novelties, and he is open-minded and eager to learn about new technologies and frameworks. He has reviewed several books and video courses published by Apress and Packt.

Acknowledgments

Whenever you see a professional doing astonishing things or being a bit above the average, remember that it's simply hard work. Nothing else. Talent helps, coincidences might happen, luck is possible. But for 99% of people, none of these things work. Hard work is the key.

I'd like to thank my family first for understanding that projects like this, along with the daily work on code, require a lot more time than just 9-to-5. I really appreciate silent nights at the computer.

Also, again, the team at Apress was very helpful during this project, with the right mixture of time and pressure to get it done on schedule. Thank you all for the opportunity to write about a subject I really care about a lot.

Sometimes it's hard, but there is always a way to see things positively. Even the biggest catastrophes may have an upside. Looking straight into the darkness might make it hard to see this. But there is one, for sure. This book and the library code used as the foundation were written during the pandemic in 2020. The upside was the leisure time not spent with friends, at holidays, or other activities. Not good, of course, but some new things learned, some pieces tried, some more lines written…you get the idea, I hope.

Introduction

This book explains Web Components. Additionally, it shows how to create a simple and small layer (a so-called thin library) around the native HTML 5 API to make your life as a developer a lot easier. This library is available as an open source project called @nyaf (Not Yet Another Framework). It's not a requirement, but it significantly reduces the hurdles for using Web Components and avoids the jump into full-blown frameworks and libraries such as Angular or React.

Who Should Read This Book?

This book is aimed at both beginners and experienced web developers. The code is mainly TypeScript. A few examples are pure ECMAScript.

In any case, I tried not to ask any prerequisites or conditions of the reader. You do not need to be a computer scientist or in perfect command of a language; you don't need to know rocket science. No matter in what context you have encountered Web Components, you should be able to read this text. However, the most benefit from this book gets everybody already working on front-end stuff. Those overwhelmed with frameworks, techniques, and monstrous project structures will learn what modern web development has to offer. Nowadays all modern browsers are able to execute ES2015 and above natively, and transpilers such as Babel or TypeScript make it easy to adapt.

Using the Code

To use the code in the book, you need the following:

- A machine with NodeJs v10+ installed. Any desktop OS will do it, whether as Windows, MacOS, or Linux. Windows users can use any shell, WSL or CMD, or PowerShell. Of course, any shell on Linux is good enough, too.

- An editor to enter code. I recommend using Visual Studio Code. It runs on all mentioned operating systems. Webstorm is also an amazingly powerful editor.

- A folder where the project is created. This is easy enough, but keep your environment clean and organized like a pro.

This book comes with a lot of examples and demo code. They are available on GitHub at `https://github.com/joergkrause/webcomponent-book`. The folders are structured following the book, chapter by chapter.

If you're relatively new to the web development field, test your knowledge by cloning the repo, bringing the examples to life, and watching the outcome. Read the text and add your own stuff once you know that the environment is up and running.

The Mission

I have years of experience with Web Components. After several projects, smaller and bigger ones, my frustration was growing over the lack of support for simple tasks and the burden of huge frameworks that intentionally solve these burdens but come with an overwhelming amount of additional features. None of the frameworks felt right. I suspected that most developer support code has a similar trigger, so I decided to start my own library project.

A full description is available in the Appendix. The project's home is `https://nyaf.comzept.de`. It's open sourced under the MIT license and available on GitHub at `https://github.com/joergkrause/nyaf`.

Now I'm on a mission. I want you to be able to learn the basics and avoid fat code as a fundamental part of your own work. There are some fields where it makes sense to add library stuff. Machine learning, artificial intelligence, and business intelligence are good examples. Front-end development is, honestly, not one of those fields. If you feel the need for help, then it's just because you don't know enough. That's the hard truth, but that's how it is. Once you master your field, you'll see that a lot projects sell you stuff you don't need, create dependencies, and lock you in their environments. It's business, after all. But if you become an expert, you'll unchain yourself from this stuff and this will improve the quality and elegance of your code.

CHAPTER 1

Introduction

Web Components are a set of W3C standards to make self-contained components: custom HTML-elements with their own properties and methods, encapsulated DOM, and styles. The technology is natively supported by all modern browsers and does not require a framework. The API has some quirks, though. I will explain these obstacles in great detail, but it's helpful to know that you can make your life easier. A thin wrapper library to handle common tasks is the answer. This is the purpose of the @nyaf (Not Yet Another Framework) code. A full description can be found in the Appendix. However, all examples and explanations within the book chapters are completely independent. Of course, you can use any other component library.

The author of this book is also the inventor and author of the @nyaf thin library.

The Global Picture

This section describes a set of modern standards for *Web Components*.

As of now, these standards are under development. Some features are well-supported and integrated into the modern HTML/DOM standard, while others are still in draft stage. You can try the examples in any browser, but Google Chrome is probably the most up to date with these features. I guess that's because Google fellows are behind many of the related specifications.

© Jörg Krause 2021
J. Krause, *Developing Web Components with TypeScript*, https://doi.org/10.1007/978-1-4842-6840-7_1

Components

The whole component idea is nothing new. It's used in many frameworks and elsewhere. Before we move onto implementation details, let's consider how the internals of a page in a browser are described. You have a tree of simple elements, defined by the language HyperText Markup Language (HTML). You also have the ability to describe the appearance of each element using Cascading Style Sheets (CSS). You have the ability to manipulate both parts dynamically at runtime using ECMAScript (also known as JavaScript). The most important point in this description is the word "tree." Elements form a tree, where one or more elements are the children of another one.

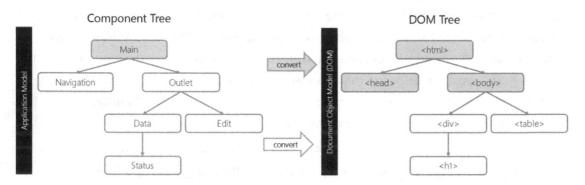

Figure 1-1. *The basic appearance of elements in the DOM*

If the basic structure of a page is already a tree of smaller parts (see Figure 1-1), it makes sense and simplifies development if on a higher level the elements form a tree too. Such a unit, hierarchical collections of functionality that can form a tree, is called a *component*.

A page hence consists of many components. Each component, in its turn, has many smaller details inside. In the end, it's still pure HTML.

The components can be very complex, sometimes more complicated than the website itself. How are such complex units created? Which principles can you borrow to make your development reliable and scalable (or at least close to it)?

Component Architecture

The well-known rule for developing complex software is: don't make complex software. If something becomes complex, split it into simpler parts and connect them in the most obvious way. A good architect is the one who can make the complex simple to handle for the developer. (That's not the same as an UX designer, who makes the complex application simple to use for the end user; that's an entirely different story.)

You can split user interfaces into visual components: each of them has its own place on the page, can "do" a well-described task, and is separate from the others.

Let's take a look at a website (see Figure 1-2), for example Twitter:

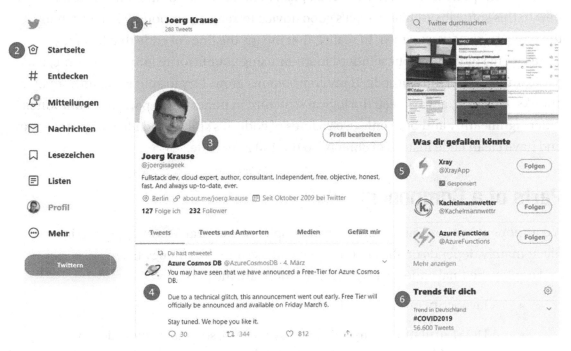

Figure 1-2. *Top level components of a complex view*

1. Top navigation

2. Main menu

3. User profile

4. Tweet feed

5. Suggestions

6. Trending subjects

Components may have sub-components. For example, messages may be part of a higher-level "message list" component, a clickable user picture itself may be a component, and so on. It boils down to HTML eventually. If there is no more

3

simplification, a native element forms a leaf in the tree. The profile branch may end with an <img> tag, then.

How do you decide what a component is? That comes from intuition, experience, and common sense. Usually it's a separate visual entity that you can describe in terms of what it does and how it interacts with the page. In the case above, the page has blocks, each of them plays its own role, and it's logical to make these components. If you're new to this software architecture, it's good advice to keep a component smaller than the typical size of your screen. In reality, that means the lines of code that form the component shall fit on your standard monitor using your favorite font size. For me, it's a maximum of 100 lines of code. If my components grow, I try to split them into smaller chunks. However, always keep the logical structure in mind. If two parts of a component differ significantly and both only use 25 lines of code, it's still a good idea to split them up and have clean code instead of clinging to the 100 lines[1] rule.

Parts of a Component

A component has several parts. They can be split into several files or appear in just one file. It mainly depends on the environment you use and the strategy to create, compile, and deploy the final code. In a logical view, these are the parts:

- A JavaScript or TypeScript class

- A DOM structure, managed solely by its class, so outside code doesn't access it (the "encapsulation" principle)

- CSS styles, applied to the component, which can be isolated or global

- An API (events, class methods, etc.) that interacts with other components or application parts

Once again, the whole "component" thing is nothing special. It's just a clever approach to handle the complexity of web pages in a way an average human being can understand.

---

[1] A single logical unit shall never have more than 100 lines of code (comments and empty lines included).

Nowadays we're forced to write very specific stuff in a general purpose language (such as TypeScript, C#, or even Java). This makes things more challenging than necessary because before we have components we need to have a "function" or a "class." I believe that someday we'll work with a more distinct domain-specific language. CSS and HTML are such domains already, and getting something similar on the code level is just a matter of time.

There exist many frameworks and development methodologies to build them, each with its own bells and whistles. Usually, special CSS classes and conventions are used to provide the "component feel" such as CSS scoping and DOM encapsulation. "Web components" provide built-in browser capabilities for that, so we don't have to emulate them anymore. They're one of the most powerful developments in recent years in the realm of web development. Unfortunately, the "component frameworks," especially Angular, Vue, and React, seem to be seen by developers as the final solution, the sole way to create components. We understand that's because it brings users and makes the framework more useful. But it's not entirely true. The native stuff is almost as good as these frameworks, as you will see soon. However, don't ask an Angular fellow. What should they say?

Web Components bring some basic features that make them so extraordinarily useful:

- Custom elements to define custom HTML elements

- A Shadow DOM to create an internal DOM for the component, hidden from the other parts of the app

- CSS scoping to declare styles that only apply inside the Shadow DOM of the component

- Event retargeting and other minor stuff to make custom components better fit the development requirements

In the next chapters, I'll go into details of such components, the fundamentals and well-supported features of web components that are really good on their own. Also, some smart stuff written around it will be explained to show how you can work very closely on the comfort level of Angular or React without actually using them.

The Rise of Thin Libraries

After digging deeper into the Web Components world, it seems that there is no need for a full framework like Angular or React anymore. However, some repeated tasks are boring and error-prone. Hence a small layer around the basic API would be helpful. That was the beginning of the @nyaf thin library. It's not called a framework because even with two more modules that became part of the package it's very small, indeed. These additional modules are first @nyaf/forms that are responsible for bidirectional binding and validation. Second, the @nyaf/store module is a simple yet powerful Flux-based store. It simplifies the architecture of huge applications dramatically.

One of the clear approaches from the beginning was the avoidance of dependencies. You need this and nothing more. Another approach is the interaction with any existing library. Even pure jQuery code will not harm the usage of @nyaf. And, finally, it's pure ES2015+ and there are no polyfills or additions for older browsers. Modern browsers have a market share of 96% and that's what you target. The full documentation is in the Appendix to this book for your reference.

It says about itself: "Write front-end apps without the hassle of a complex framework, use the full power of HTML 5, and keep a component-based style."

Single-Page Apps

A single-page application (SPA) is a web application or website that consists of a single page, usually called index.html, that is loaded into the web browser. The web browser loads some code and executes it then. The code interacts with the web browser by dynamically rewriting parts of web page with new data from the web server. The goal is faster transitions that make the website feel more like a native app.

In an SPA, all necessary HTML, JavaScript, and CSS code is either retrieved by the browser as one additional request, or the appropriate resources are dynamically loaded and added to the page as necessary, usually in response to user actions. The page does not reload at any point in the process, nor does control transfer to another page. The location hash part of the URL or the HTML5 History API can be used to provide navigation capabilities within the application.

Web Components make it easy to create SPAs. The main part is a feature called a *router*. The router routes a navigation action (usually a click on a hyperlink or button) by using an assigned URL to some kind of management code. That code creates a new tree of components and moves it to a particular target element. The browser reacts to this operation by rendering the elements. The developer has to make these decisions to get it working:

1. Define a target, an element where the replaceable tree appears. This is called an *outlet*.

2. Create a definition that maps routes to components. This is a *router configuration*.

Again, some convenient stuff can be created to make your daily life easier. See Chapter 8 for more details of possible implementations.

The HTML 5 API

The HTML 5 API is amazingly powerful and covers a wide range of features. All existing frameworks and libraries—with no exception—are built on top of this API. The advantage of using a certain framework is primarily that you get a simplified view, a reduced view, a more elegant API style, or even more robust code made by additional error handling. These are all good reasons to use a framework or library, right?

Imagine you know all these APIs. What would happen is that you can avoid few of the libraries and probably a whole framework. The code is finally smaller, faster, and easier to maintain. Learning the HTML 5 API is essential for web developers nowadays.

The HTML 5 API is fundamental for web developers. Learn it first and keep it a reference all the time. I recommend MDN (Mozilla Developer Network) as documentation.

The Template Language

A template language simplifies the creation of forms. It's not enforced; you can of course use the basic API and pure HTML. In complex applications, you'll see that there is a lot of repeating code. There are many template languages available and I'll present a few of them so you can compare and choose freely.

Smart Decorators

Instead of splitting the definition and registration, the component itself covers all necessary information as metadata. Decorators are a feature of the TypeScript compiler and eventually they will become part of the ECMAScript standard.

This coding style supports the "separation of concerns" principle and is easy to implement. A final solution could look like this (the thin library shown in the Appendix implements this feature, but it's quite easy to make such enhancements in your own code to simplify your life as a developer):

```
@CustomElement('app-main')
export class MainComponent extends BaseComponent<{}> {

  protected render() {
    return (<h1>Demo</h1>);
  }
}
```

The decorator `CustomElement` is called in the instantiation process of the class. It can access both the underlying function definition and the instance. Here you can manipulate the code further (at runtime) by adding hidden properties, for example. Other code fragments may access these properties and act according to these hidden instructions. In the above example, some external code may see this and take it as a "please register me" instruction. The advantage here is that the component developer doesn't need to think about such infrastructure stuff and the code is much smaller and easier to read.

TypeScript

TypeScript is not covered in this book. It is, however, the language used to write components and related libraries. It's not exactly necessary for writing Web Components, but it's a strong tool in a developer's toolset. The ability to transform JSX has already been explained, and if you don't use TypeScript you have to replace one tool with another. So avoiding it gains nothing, while embracing it offers a bunch of advantages.

One of the main reasons for its success is that valid JavaScript is valid TypeScript. Any ES2015 example shown here will be accepted by the TypeScript transpiler. What's added is the ability to use features from newer JavaScript versions such as ECMAScript 2020 today, even if the browser does not have full support yet. And it adds types that reduce error-prone code. In short, it is this:

TYPESCRIPT = JAVASCRIPT + TYPE SYSTEM

TypeScript is compatible with ECMAScript[2] 2018 and provides necessary polyfills.

WebPack

WebPack is an open-source JavaScript module bundler. It was primarily developed for JavaScript, but it can transform almost all front-end assets like HTML, CSS, and images if the corresponding plug-ins (called loaders) are included. WebPack takes modules with dependencies and generates static assets representing those modules. The dependencies are investigated and used to generate a dependency graph. This allows web developers to use a modular approach for their development purposes. WebPack can be used from the command line or can be configured using a configuration file named `webpack.config.js`[3]. The configuration file is the most common approach and uses JavaScript to define an object with all required settings.

WebPack is highly extensible via rules that allow developers to write custom tasks that they want to perform when bundling files together. NodeJs is required for using WebPack, hence it's a command line tool running at development time. WebPack can add loading capabilities to the bundle it creates that may make the final code a bit bigger than the pure application code requires.

---

[2]The official name of JavaScript is ECMAScript.
[3]This is the default name. You can use any name if you like.

Compatibility

For every new technology it takes some time until all browsers and tools have a fully working implementation. The great news about the year 2020 is that meanwhile all browsers (see Figure 1-3) have full support and you rarely need a polyfill.

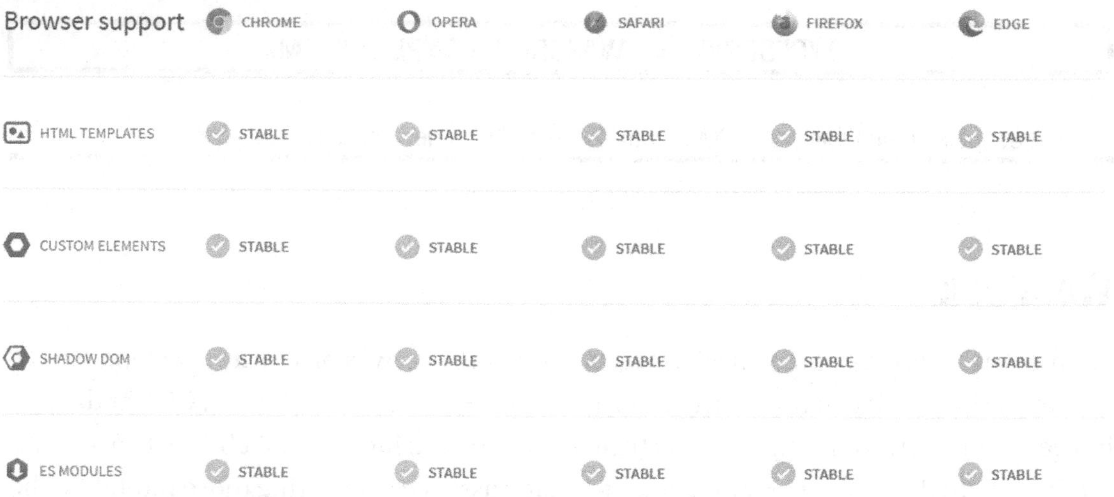

Browser support	CHROME	OPERA	SAFARI	FIREFOX	EDGE
HTML TEMPLATES	STABLE	STABLE	STABLE	STABLE	STABLE
CUSTOM ELEMENTS	STABLE	STABLE	STABLE	STABLE	STABLE
SHADOW DOM	STABLE	STABLE	STABLE	STABLE	STABLE
ES MODULES	STABLE	STABLE	STABLE	STABLE	STABLE

Figure 1-3. Compatibility chart from the webcomponents.org website

Other Libraries

Apart from the one I feature in this book, `@nyaf`, there are few other libraries that I found worth mentioning here. They differ in focus and quality. It depends on your project and feature requirements which one suits better. It's also a good idea to analyze them and learn how things work internally and consider going with some code where you have the ownership. The following list is pulled from `webcomponents.org`:

- **Hybrids** is a UI library for creating Web Components with a simple and functional API. The library uses plain objects and pure functions for defining custom elements, which allow very flexible composition. It provides a built-in cache mechanism, a template engine based on tagged template literals, and integration with developer tools.

- **LitElement** uses lit-html to render into the element's Shadow DOM and adds an API to help manage element properties and attributes. LitElement reacts to changes in properties and renders declaratively using lit-html.

- **Polymer** is a Web Component library built by Google, with a simple element creation API. Polymer offers one- and two-way data binding into element templates and provides shims for better cross-browser performance.

- **Skate.js** is a library built on top of the W3C Web Component specs that enables you to write functional and performant Web Components with a very small footprint. Skate is inherently cross-framework compatible. For example, it works seamlessly with—and complements—React and other frameworks.

- **Slim.js** is a lightweight Web Component library that provides extended capabilities for components, such as data binding, using ES2015 native class inheritance. This library is focused on providing the developer the ability to write robust and native Web Components without the hassle of dependencies and an overhead of a framework.

- **Stencil** is an open source compiler that generates standards-compliant Web Components.

Summary

This chapter provided a first introduction in the world of Web Components, the way they work, and what to do with them. I also captured the browser support and some libraries that can be used to boost productivity in connection with Web Components.

CHAPTER 2

Making Components

You can create a custom HTML element, described by a class, with its own methods and properties, events and so on. Once a custom element is defined, you can use it on par with built-in HTML elements. **These elements are called Web Components.**

Basics

Such a simple way to extend the vocabulary of HTML makes your life as a developer easier. The HTML dictionary is rich, but not infinite. There are no `<easy-tabs>`, `<sliding-carousel>`, or `<beautiful-upload>`. Just think of any other tag you might need. But the crucial part here is that you can avoid using a JavaScript framework entirely and still get a foundation for a solid architecture of an front-end application. Web Components need some code, though.

You can define them with a special class, and then use them as if they were always a part of HTML.

There are two kinds of custom elements:

- Autonomous custom elements are custom elements that extend the abstract `HTMLElement` class.

- Customized built-in elements extend built-in elements, like a customized button, based on `HTMLButtonElement`, etc.

First I'll cover autonomous elements and then customized built-in ones.

To create a custom element, you need to tell the browser several details about it: how to show it, what to do when the element is added or removed to the page, etc. That's done by making a class with special methods. That's easy, as there are only a few methods, and all of them are optional.

© Jörg Krause 2021
J. Krause, *Developing Web Components with TypeScript*, https://doi.org/10.1007/978-1-4842-6840-7_2

A sketch with the full list is shown in Listing 2-1.

Listing 2-1. Simple Component (chapter2/component/component.js)

```js
class MyElement extends HTMLElement {
  constructor() {
    super();
    // element created
  }

  connectedCallback() {
    this.innerHTML = '<h1>Hello Web Component</h1>';
    // called when the element is added to the document
  }

  disconnectedCallback() {
    // called when the element is removed from the document
  }

  static get observedAttributes() {
    return [
      /* array of attribute names to monitor for changes */
    ];
  }

  attributeChangedCallback(name, oldValue, newValue) {
    // called when one of attributes listed above is modified
  }

  adoptedCallback() {
    // called when moved to a new document
  }

  // there can be other element methods and properties
}
```

All methods shown are optional, so implement only those you really need. Be aware that under certain circumstances the methods might be called multiple times.

After defining the component, you need to register it as an element. You need to let the browser know that <my-element> is served by your new class.

```
customElements.define('my-element', MyElement);
```

Now for any HTML elements with the tag <my-element> an instance of MyElement is created, and the aforementioned methods are called. You also can use document. createElement('my-element') to create the element through an HTML 5 API call and attach the element later to the DOM.

A custom element name must have a hyphen, so *my-element* and *super-button* are valid names, but *myelement* is not.

The writing style with hyphens is also called kebab-style[1]. It's used to ensure that there are no name conflicts between built-in and custom HTML elements.

To load and use the component, you need an HTML page. This can be as simple as the code shown in Listing 2-2.

Listing 2-2. Start Page (chapter2/component/index.html)

```html
<!DOCTYPE html>
<html lang="en">
  <head>
    <meta charset="UTF-8" />
    <meta name="viewport"
          content="width=device-width, initial-scale=1.0" />
    <title>Document</title>
    <script src="component.js"></script>
  </head>
  <body>
    <my-element></my-element>
  </body>
</html>
```

---

[1]See Wikipedia for details about the origin of this term. In short, it's meat on a skewer. The letters are the meat and the dashes are the skewer.

It's recommended to wait for the document ready state before applying for registration. This might or might not change the behavior; it depends on the inner construction of the component's content. But waiting for the ready event seems to fix some common issues and has rarely any disadvantages.

A First Example

For example, there already exists a `<time>` element in HTML for date and time information. But it doesn't do any formatting by itself.

Let's create a `<time-format>` element that displays the time in a nice, language-aware format, as shown in Listing 2-3.

Listing 2-3. Time and Date Component (chapter2/time/time.js)

```
class TimeFormat extends HTMLElement {

  connectedCallback() {
    let date = new Date(this.getAttribute('datetime')
               || Date.now());

    this.innerHTML = new Intl.DateTimeFormat('default', {
      year: this.getAttribute('year') || undefined,
      month: this.getAttribute('month') || undefined,
      day: this.getAttribute('day') || undefined,
      hour: this.getAttribute('hour') || undefined,
      minute: this.getAttribute('minute') || undefined,
      second: this.getAttribute('second') || undefined,
      timeZoneName: this.getAttribute('time-zone-name')
               || undefined,
    }).format(date);
  }
}

customElements.define('time-format', TimeFormat);
```

To use it, the piece of HTML in Listing 2-4 is necessary.

Listing 2-4. Usage of Date Component (chapter2/time/index.html)

```
<time-format
  datetime="2020-04-13"
  year="numeric"
  month="long"
  day="numeric"
  hour="numeric"
  minute="numeric"
  second="numeric"
  time-zone-name="short"
></time-format>
```

The class has only one method, `connectedCallback()`. The browser calls it when a `<time-format>` element is added to the document and it uses the built-in `Intl.DateTimeFormat`[2] data formatter, well-supported across the browsers, to show a nicely formatted time. You need to register your new element by `customElements.define(tag, class)` and then you can use it everywhere. The output is shown in Figure 2-1.

13. April 2020, 2:00:00 MESZ

Figure 2-1. *Output of the component in German form*

Observing Unset Elements

If the browser encounters any `<time-format>` elements before `customElements.define` gets called, it will not produce an error. The element is yet unknown, just like any non-standard tag. It will render into nothing. That's hard to capture. To make it visible, you could add a style that uses the pseudo CSS selector `:not(:defined)`.

When `customElement.define` is called, the element is "upgraded." A new instance of the `TimeFormat` class is created for each element, and the `connectedCallback` method is called. The element becomes `:defined` then.

---

[2]This requires ECMAScript 2015 support, which is browser native. Be aware of this in case you have an environment that still downgrades to ES5 for some historical reason.

Upgrade   The term "upgrade" makes sense because the process might
be delayed. You can add custom elements to a document, and the browser
might ignore them. Then, at any time, you can call the `define` method.
The browser will now remember the formerly ignored elements and call the
`connectedCallback()` method. Whatever happens in there will render on
screen. The element is now upgraded to being a component. The upgrading
happens in document order.

A very helpful stylesheet to achieve the visibility of not-yet-upgraded components is
shown in Listing 2-5.

Listing 2-5.   Style the Host (chapter2/undefined/index.html)

```
<style>
  :not(:defined) {
    display: block;
    width: 150px;
    border-bottom: 2px dotted red;
    text-align: center;
  }
  :not(:defined):before {
    content: "unknown element !";
    color: red;
  }
</style>
```

In this example, the JavaScript part is missing (to simulate an error) and hence the
style makes the element visible. The result is shown in Figure 2-2.

unknown element !

Figure 2-2.   *Output for an unknown element*

Custom Elements AP

To get information about custom elements, there are two helpful methods:

- `customElements.get(name)` returns the class for a custom element with the given name.

- `customElements.whenDefined(name)` returns a promise that resolves (without value) when a custom element with the given name becomes upgraded.

You can't get information about regular HTML elements, such as a button, using these methods.

It's important to start the rendering in `connectedCallback`, not in the constructor. In the example above, element content is rendered (created) that way. The constructor is not suitable. When the constructor is called, it's too early. The element is created, but the browser did not yet process and assign attributes at this stage. For instance, calls to `getAttribute` would return `null`.

An additional reason is performance. In the further stages of the render process, some code might decide not to render the element or replace the render content with some message. Imagine a grid, which might become huge, but due to some attribute setting it's replaced by a "too many data" message. Processing all attributes first and rendering then makes sense.

The `connectedCallback` method triggers when the element is added to the document—not just appended to another element as a child, but actually becomes a part of the page. So you can build a detached DOM, create elements, and prepare them for later use. They will only be actually rendered when they make it into the page. In the first examples, that's always the case because the element is written directly into the page. However, in a more dynamic environment, such as a single-page app (SPA), this would not be the same.

Observing Attributes

In the current implementation of <time-format>, after the element is rendered, further attribute changes don't have any effect. That's strange for an HTML element. Usually, when we change an attribute, like href of an anchor element, we expect the change to be immediately visible. All kinds of effects and animations need this behavior.

We can observe attributes by providing their list in the observedAttributes() method. It's static (not part of the prototype) because it's global definition once for all instances of the element. For such attributes, the method attributeChangedCallback is called when they are modified. It doesn't trigger any other attribute for performance reasons.

Listing 2-6 shows a new <time-format> version that auto-updates when attributes change.

Listing 2-6. Using Observed Attributes (chapter2/observed/time.js)

```
class TimeFormat extends HTMLElement {

  render() {
    let date = new Date(this.getAttribute('datetime')
               || Date.now());

    this.innerHTML = new Intl.DateTimeFormat("default", {
      year: this.getAttribute('year') || undefined,
      month: this.getAttribute('month') || undefined,
      day: this.getAttribute('day') || undefined,
      hour: this.getAttribute('hour') || undefined,
      minute: this.getAttribute('minute') || undefined,
      second: this.getAttribute('second') || undefined,
      timeZoneName: this.getAttribute('time-zone-name')
               || undefined,
    }).format(date);
  }

  connectedCallback() {
    if (!this.rendered) {
      this.render();
      this.rendered = true;
```

```
    }
  }

  static get observedAttributes() {
    return ['datetime', 'year', 'month', 'day', 'hour',
            'minute', 'second', 'time-zone-name'];
  }

  attributeChangedCallback(name, oldValue, newValue) {
    this.render();
  }

}

customElements.define("time-format", TimeFormat);
```

The usage doesn't look much different from the first example.

```
<time-format id="elem"
             hour="numeric"
             minute="numeric"
             second="numeric">
</time-format>
```

However, when you change one of the observed attributes in your code, the element re-renders automatically:

```
const elem = document.querySelector('time-format');
setInterval(
  () => elem.setAttribute('datetime', new Date()),
  1000
);
```

The rendering logic is moved to the render() helper method. You call it once when the element is inserted into the document. After a change of an attribute, listed in observedAttributes(), the method attributeChangedCallback triggers and re-renders the element. The call to the render method must be implemented in the component. On the first look, there's not much magic here and, in comparison with frameworks such as Angular or React, it might feel primitive. But the ability to control the rendering and have a clear cycle makes the implementation very handy and straightforward.

Attribute Data

The component itself can handle only scalar values. This means you're limited to
string, boolean, and number. Anything else will run through toString() and may end
up as something like [Object object] or, in case of null as a string "null". That's a
lot weaker than the binding we can see in Angular, for example. Of course, a private
implementation can detect such types and use JSON.stringify and JSON.parse. That is,
indeed, the slowest but most robust way to serialize complex data.

In the @nyaf thin library, the JSON methods are used to transport complex data. In
all other situations, you must implement your own mechanism. A publish-subscribe
pattern or something based on observers is often a better and more efficient way
to get complex data into components.

Another way is to ditch the usage of observed attributes completely and use a
programmatic way. This will, however, limit the component to be accessible by code
only. That's a serious limitation indeed, but let's explore an example (Listing 2-7) anyway
to give you the idea.

Listing 2-7. Programmatic Attribute Access (chapter2/attributes/objects.js)

```
class ObjectComponent extends HTMLElement {

  render() {
    this.innerHTML = null;
    const pre = document.createElement('pre');
    pre.innerHTML = JSON.stringify(this.content);
    this.insertAdjacentElement('afterbegin', pre);
  }

  connectedCallback() {
    this.render();
  }

  static get observedAttributes() {
    return ['content'];
  }
```

```
attributeChangedCallback(name, oldValue, newValue) {
  this.content = newValue;
  this.render();
}

set content(value) {
  this._content = value;
  this.render();
}

get content() {
  return this._content;
}

}

document.addEventListener('readystatechange', (docEvent) => {
  if (document.readyState === 'complete') {
    customElements.define("obj-element", ObjectComponent);

    document.querySelector('button')
            .addEventListener('click', (e) => {
      document.querySelector('obj-element').content = {
        type: 'object'
      };
    });
  }
});
```

The key is line 19 with access to the custom property content. Here we assign an object and call the render method immediately. That bypasses the conversion to string type and keeps the stringifyer working as expected. Figure 2-3 shows the expected result.

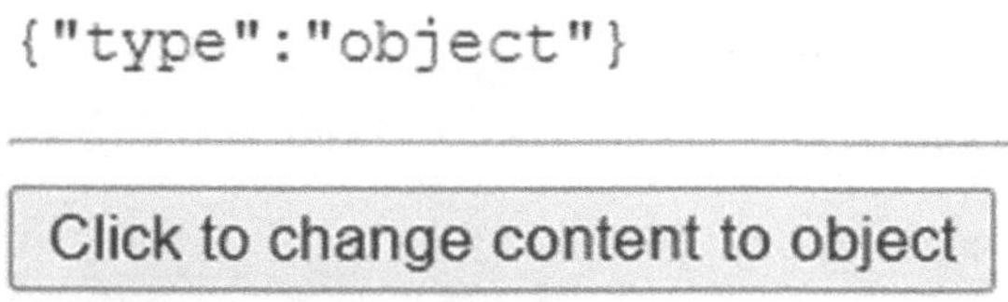

```
{"type":"object"}
```

Click to change content to object

Figure 2-3. *Transfering objects into a component*

The observation is still present to allow a static value for initialization (see Listing 2-8).

Listing 2-8. Programmatic Attribute Access (chapter2/attributes/index.html)

```
<obj-element content="Default String Content"></obj-element>
<hr>
<button type="button" >Click to change content to object</button>
```

Discussing the Options

To monitor external data without the ability to use the observation, you may also consider using a `Proxy` object and optionally the `MutationObserver` class. Both ways use ES 2015 classes and are hence native APIs. A `Proxy` gives you the ability to intercept the access to an object's properties. Whatever and whenever some outside code accesses a property, a callback is called. This can be used to trigger the `render` method.

The MutationObserver Type

A `MutationObserver`, on the other hand, monitors the DOM itself and calls a callback if something changes. However, this function runs in a microtask and is not entirely synchronous. That means the new attribute value (if observed) may not have the current value already. To avoid non-deterministic behavior, the `MutationRecord` instance that the callback returns will not give access to the new value. Of course, there are several ways to patch the prototype or add an interceptor, but it all feels hackish and not very reliable. The biggest risk is that the API will change internally without any notification and the code will fail eventually out of nowhere with a simple browser update. I made some experiments with this and never found a satisfying solution. If you want to dig deeper into this, the code snippet in Listing 2-9 gives you the general usage of such an observer.

Listing 2-9. Excerpt from the Mutation Demo (chapter2/mutation/objects.js)

```
document.addEventListener('readystatechange', (docEvent) => {
  if (document.readyState === 'complete') {

    const observer = new MutationObserver(mutations => {
      console.log('mutations', mutations);
    });

    customElements.define("obj-element", ObjectComponent);

    document.querySelector('button')
            .addEventListener('click', (e) => {
      // observed by MutationObserver
      document.querySelector('obj-element').setAttribute('content',
      { type: 'object' });
    });
    // just observe the attributes
    observer.observe(
      document.querySelector('obj-element'),
      { attributes: true }
    );
  }
});
```

Proxy

A Proxy class is pure JavaScript and handles just an object. But a Web Component is an object, so this sounds like a feasible solution. However, the amount of boilerplate code is significant. In a real-life scenario, you would move this to a base class, but the example shows nonetheless the weakness of HTML 5 API (and its power, too). See Listing 2-10.

Listing 2-10. Attribute Handling with a Proxy (chapter2/proxy/objects.js)

```
class ObjectComponent extends HTMLElement {
  constructor() {
    super();
    this.proxy = new Proxy( this, {
      get: () => { return this.content; },
```

```
      set: (target, prop, value) => {
       this._content = value;
       if (ObjectComponent.observedAttributes.includes(prop)) {
          this.setAttribute(prop, JSON.stringify(value));
       }
       return true;
      }
    });
  }
  render() {
    this.innerHTML = null;
    const pre = document.createElement('pre');
    pre.innerHTML = JSON.stringify(this.content);
    this.insertAdjacentElement('afterbegin', pre);
  }
  connectedCallback() { this.render(); }
  static get observedAttributes() { return ['content']; }
  attributeChangedCallback(name, oldValue, newValue) {
    if (!oldValue) {
      this.setAttribute('content', JSON.stringify(newValue));
    }
    if (oldValue !== newValue) { this.render(); }
  }
  set content(value) { this.proxy.content = value; }
  get content() {
    return JSON.parse(this.getAttribute('content'));
  }
}
document.addEventListener('readystatechange',
  (docEvent) => {
    if (document.readyState === 'complete') {
      customElements.define("obj-element", ObjectComponent);
      document.querySelector('button')
        .addEventListener('click', (e) => {
```

```
      document.querySelector('obj-element').content = {
        type: 'object'
      };
    });
  }
});
```

Again, there is no way to use the programmatic access here:

```
document.querySelector('obj-element').content = ...
```

Because the attribute observation is still operational, the external access from HTML would work too. Insofar it does exactly what's expected. The external access and the programmatic access both write into the property content. That's observed by the proxy handler's setter path. Here we look at what's really an observed attribute (line 10) and trigger the regular attribute observer (line 11). The difference is that the value received by the proxy is still an object (while the internal API has to call toString first and delivers [Object object]). Now we can transform it into the stringified version and store this in the attribute. The actual render code expects an object (line 21). To make it work and make use of the JSON.parse method to return an actual object in a transparent way, the getter method at the end (line 47) transforms the string back.

Proxy objects are amazingly powerful, but dealing with them is sort of tricky. Test your code carefully, watch the flow in the debugger, and try to simplify a solution as much as possible once it's running.

Rendering Order

When the browser's HTML parser builds the DOM, elements are processed one after another, parents before children. Imagine you have something like

```
<outer-element><inner-element></inner-element></outer-element>
```

Then an <outer-element> element is created and connected to DOM first, and then an <inner-element>.

This leads to important consequences for custom elements. For example, if a custom element tries to access `innerHTML` in `connectedCallback`, it gets nothing:

```
customElements.define(
  'user-info',
  class extends HTMLElement {
    connectedCallback() {
      alert(this.innerHTML);
    }
  }
);
<user-info>Joerg</user-info>
```

If you run it, the alert is empty. That's because there are no children on that stage, so the DOM is unfinished. HTML parser connected the custom element `<user-info>` and is going to proceed to its children, but they're not here yet.

If you like to pass information to custom elements, you can use attributes. They are available immediately.

Be careful when trying to reproduce. The effect is visible if you define the element first and use the code later (the script tag comes before HTML). If you let the browser parse the HTML first and "upgrade" the component by executing the script later, the content is already processed and it works as expected. Delaying access is the key.

Delaying Access

If you really need the content immediately, you can defer access to it with a zero-delay `setTimeout`:

```
<script>
customElements.define('user-info', class extends HTMLElement {

  connectedCallback() {
    setTimeout(() => alert(this.innerHTML));
  }
```

```
});
</script>
```

```
<user-info>Joerg</user-info>
```

Now the alert shows "Joerg" because you run it asynchronously and the HTML parsing is complete. Of course, this solution is not perfect. If nested custom elements also use setTimeout to initialize themselves, then they queue up: the outer setTimeout triggers first, and then the inner one. And that's simply the wrong order.

Let's demonstrate that with an example:

```
<script>
customElements.define('user-info', class extends HTMLElement {
  connectedCallback() {
    console.log(`${this.id} connected.`);
    setTimeout(() => console.log(`${this.id} initialized.`));
  }
});
</script>
```

```
<user-info id="outer">
  <user-info id="inner"></user-info>
</user-info>
```

Output order:

- outer connected

- inner connected

- outer initialized

- inner initialized

You can clearly see that the outer element finishes initialization before the inner one.

There's no built-in callback that triggers after nested elements are ready. If needed, you can implement such things on your own. For instance, inner elements can dispatch events like initialized, and outer ones can listen and react to them.

Introducing a Life Cycle

The current implementation of a Web Component is very simple. This makes it easy to get in the first step, but some additional implementation effort is required. One idea to solve the issues with the last example is to introduce a loading callback. Once the render stage has passed, the component fires an event or—even better—resolves a Promise. The outer component can't wait for this to happen and proceeds once the children confirm they are done. Again, a not-so-good working example:

```
class OuterElement extends HTMLElement {
  constructor() {
   super();
   console.log('outer ctor');
  }
  connectedCallback() {
    console.log('outer render');
    this.innerHTML = '<h1>Hello Web Component</h1>' +
                     this.innerHTML +
                     '<hr>';
  }
}
class InnerElement extends HTMLElement {

  constructor() {
    super();
    console.log('inner ctor');
  }
  connectedCallback() {
    console.log('inner render');
    this.innerHTML = 'Inner Part';
  }
}
customElements.define('outer-element', OuterElement); customElements.
define('inner-element', InnerElement);
```

Let's assume a piece of HTML like this:

```
<outer-element>
  <inner-element></inner-element>
</outer-element>
```

The expected render output would be this one:

```
<h1>Hello Web Component</h1><small>Inner Part</small><hr>
```

If you execute this "as is," the result is wrong, as shown in Figure 2-4.

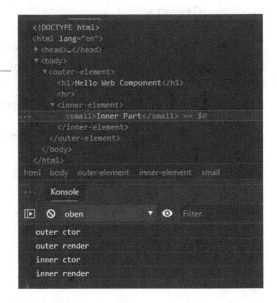

Figure 2-4. *Wrong order in rendered HTML*

Look at the DOM. The `<inner-element>` comes after the `<hr>`, which is not what you expected.

So, how could you make the outer component wait for all of the children? Attaching events to the component itself isn't an option because the content might be simple static text and a text node can't trigger events.

Waiting for other custom elements would be easy. You could just loop through all outer elements, look whether they have a specific state, and wait. Also, to make it easier to handle, the render method could be async. But in case of regular HTML and static text, this will not work. One proposal is to set an explicit trigger for the render part:

```
<outer-element>
  Static Text Before
  <inner-element></inner-element>
  Static Text After
  <content-done />
</outer-element>
```

The element `<content-done />` is such a trigger. Once it occurs, it will call the render method of the outermost element. The whole code is shown in Listing 2-11.

Listing 2-11. Using a Life Cycle (chapter2/lifecycle/component.js)

```
class OuterElement extends HTMLElement {
  constructor() {
    super();
    console.log('outer ctor');
  }
  async connectedCallback() {
    console.log('outer render');
  }
  render() {
    console.log('ready to go');
    this.innerHTML = '<h1>Hello Web Component</h1>' +
                      this.innerHTML +
                      '<hr>';
  }
}
class InnerElement extends HTMLElement {
  constructor() {
    super();
    console.log('inner ctor');
  }
```

```
  connectedCallback() {
    console.log('inner render');
    this.innerHTML = 'Inner Part';
  }
}
customElements.define('outer-element', OuterElement); customElements.
define('inner-element', InnerElement);
// the currently needed utility
customElements.define('content-done',
    class extends HTMLElement {
      connectedCallback() {
        const {parentElement} = this;
        parentElement.removeChild(this);
        if (parentElement.render) {
          parentElement.render();
        }
      }
    }
);
```

There are two critical parts here. First, the outermost element must be prepared to receive a call. In Listing 2-11, it's the custom render method. Second, the trigger element looks a bit awkward and is some context knowledge the template developer needs to have—a thing we usually try to avoid. See Figure 2-5.

Hello Web Component

Static Text Before Inner Part Static Text After

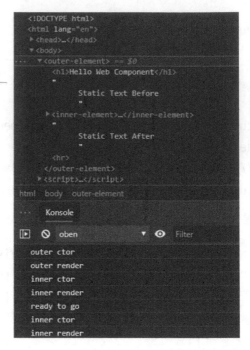

Figure 2-5. *The behavior with a trigger element*

If you watch carefully on the console output, you will see that the inner part is called twice. First is the immediate call from the render engine once the component is registered. Second is the call from the custom trigger element. While this seems in the demo not relevant, it could create a serious performance penalty in a huge and more complex application.

If you have custom components only, this render approach is much more feasible:

```
<outer-element>
  <inner-element></inner-element>
</outer-element>
```

Here the `<inner-element>` could call `render,` and if that happens for all elements, it will work smoothly. You just have to test whether the content exists to let the innermost element render itself immediately. The `@nyaf` thin library shown in the Appendix does exactly this, along with other libraries such as Polymer or Lightning.

There is discussion going on that Web Components might support this behavior by introducing a native event that is called once the content children are rendered completely.

An even better way is to wait for the elements to be available. This can be made by just delaying the component registration after the document ready event:

```
if (document.readyState === 'interactive'
|| document.readyState === 'complete') {
  customElements.define('outer-element', OuterElement);
  customElements.define('inner-element', InnerElement);
} else {
  document.addEventListener('DOMContentLoaded', _ => {
    customElements.define('outer-element', OuterElement);
    customElements.define('inner-element', InnerElement);
  });
}
```

Here the code looks for an already available ready state or the finishing event.

This works very well for an application with a static appearance. However, if you have components loaded dynamically, as happens in a SPA with router logic, this will not work. The final (and best) solution depends on the kind of app you write and may change over time.

Customized Built-in Elements

New elements that you create, such as `<time-format>`, don't have any associated semantics. They are unknown to search engines and accessibility devices can't handle them. Such things can be important, though. A search engine would be interested to know that you actually show a time. And if you're making a special kind of button, why not reuse the existing `<button>` functionality?

You can extend and customize built-in HTML elements by inheriting from their classes. For example, buttons are instances of HTMLButtonElement. Extend HTMLButtonElement with a new class:

```
class HelloButton extends HTMLButtonElement {
  /* custom element methods */
}
```

Provide a third argument to customElements.define that specifies the type to extend by using the tag's name:

```
customElements.define('hello-button', HelloButton, {extends: 'button'});
```

There may be different tags that share the same DOM-class; that's why specifying extends is needed. To get the custom element, insert a regular <button> tag, but add the is attribute to it like this:

```
<button is="hello-button">...</button>
```

Here's a full example:

```
<script>
// The button that says "hello" on click
class HelloButton extends HTMLButtonElement {
  constructor() {
    super();
    this.addEventListener('click', () => alert("Hello!"));
  }
}

customElements.define('hello-button',
                      HelloButton,
                      {extends: 'button'});
</script>

<button is="hello-button">Click me</button>

<button is="hello-button" disabled>Disabled</button>
```

The new button extends the built-in one. That means it keeps the same styles and standard features like the disabled attribute.

If you prefer using the API, especially the document.createElement method, then you'll find a second parameter that is an object with just one property, is:

```
let liComponent = document.createElement('ul', { is : 'app-list' })
```

The component itself must be registered as before, but now with the extension instruction:

```
customElements.define('app-list', ListComponent, { extends: "ul" });
```

This way you can modify any existing element and there is no need to create custom tags from scratch:

```
<ul is="app-list"></ul>
```

Compared to Angular, this is similar to a directive that expands existing components.

Advantage of TypeScript

In the previous examples, I used only pure ES2015 code. The TypeScript syntax would be similar. However, using TypeScript's features could make it even easier to handle certain tasks. One of the important parts is the handling of attributes. As already shown in the previous examples, the observedAttributes method is responsible for triggering the observation. Accessing those attributes means calling methods like this.getAttribute('name'). And here lies a culprit. The usage of strings is error-prone. A much better way is to use named properties, like this.name.

Using Generics

The key is a generic. In TypeScript, you can assign a type to a concrete type placeholder to achieve this. However, a full implementation is quite tricky and it would be nice if you can handle this internally and not bother the developer with all the details. Let's work this out step by step.

The component will ultimately look like this:

```
class TimeFormat extends BaseComponent<TimeProperties> {

  constructor() {
    super();
  }

  render() {
    let date = new Date(this.data.datetime
                || Date.now());

    this.innerHTML = new Intl.DateTimeFormat("default", {
      year: this.data.year || undefined,
      month: this.data.month || undefined,
      day: this.data.day || undefined,
      hour: this.data.hour || undefined,
      minute: this.data.minute || undefined,
      second: this.data.second || undefined,
      timeZoneName: this.data['time-zone-name']
                || undefined,
    }).format(date);
  }

  connectedCallback() {
    this.render();
  }

}
```

As you can see, the getAttribute calls are replaced by this.data calls that IntelliSense understands through the generic of the base class BaseComponent. However, this will not work because the generic is stripped out by the TypeScript transpiler and JavaScript doesn't understand that. To get the type at runtime, you need an instance of TimeProperties. The first decision to make is the type itself. It must be class because you need a runtime instance. An interface won't work here. So let's get the class:

```
class TimeProperties {
  datetime: string = '';
  year: string ='';
```

```
  month: string ='';
  day: string ='';
  hour: string ='';
  minute: string ='';
  second: string ='';
  'time-zone-name': string = '';
}
```

Then, you need to configure the base class. This involves two steps. The first is the assignment of the generic type to the property data. This is primarily for convenient access. The second is a method that retrieves the properties of the TimeProperties class and returns them as an array that observedAttributes can handle. The difficult part here is, and it's the point where the coding can be a bit weird, that this method is static while on the component you work with an instance. Static members are being initialized before instance members, and especially before the constructor gets called. Unfortunately TypeScript does not really have an elegant way to provide this, so you can mix in some JavaScript here. The result is a base class:

```
abstract class BaseComponent extends HTMLElement {
private static _keys: any; private _data: T;
constructor() { super(); this._data = {} as T; }
public get data(): T { return this._data; }
static get observedAttributes() { return (this.constructor as any)._keys ||
[]; }
attributeChangedCallback(name: string, oldValue: any, newValue: any) { if
(oldValue !== newValue) { (this.data as any)[name] = newValue; } this.
render(); }
public abstract render(): void;
}
```

The class is abstract to enforce the implementation. It's generic, as you planned it. It extends the usual HTMLElement class to make a real Web Component. The crucial part is the call to get the array of properties: return (this.constructor as any)._keys (line 17). Here you access the constructor object that's available in the static initialization phase. But how do you add the data at runtime to this property?

The trick is using a decorator. A decorator is a TypeScript feature that provides additional metadata to an object. It is static by definition and instantiated before the actual object. Technically it's just pure function calls, so you can do anything within the decorator. Decorators will become part of ECMAScript sooner or later (currently they are experimental), but due to the polyfill the TypeScript compiler creates there's no risk in using them. The head of the class will now look like this:

```
@Observes(TimeProperties)
class TimeFormat extends BaseComponent<TimeProperties> {
  // content omitted for brevity
}
```

The decorator Observes is defined like this:

```
type Type = new (...args: any[]) => T;
function Observes<T extends {}>(type: Type) {
  // the original decorator function
  internal(target: Object): void {
    Object.defineProperty(target.constructor, '_keys', {
      get: function () {
        const defaults = new type()
        return Object.keys(defaults);
      },
      enumerable: false,
      configurable: false });
  }
  // return the decorator return internal;
}
```

The inner part defines where the decorator is allowed to appear. The given signature (line 5) is for a class. The class definition itself is delivered by the infrastructure through the target parameter. On that object (internally it's a Function object) you create a dynamic property. An instance property goes to the target directly, while a static property goes to the *constructor*. Pure JavaScript magic, by the way. The strategy has nothing to do with Web Components or TypeScript. To keep TypeScript from complaining, a helper type is created, called Type. This helper defines a constructor signature to allow the code to create an actual instance (new type()). And on this actual type you can call Object.keys to get all the property names.

You have seen that the property class has initializers for the members (`datetime: string = '';`) That's necessary because otherwise the TypeScript transpiler would strip this code out to make a smaller bundle and assume that JavaScript can handle this (it can), but here you really need values at runtime and hence the initializers enforce the existence of the properties. The actual values don't matter, as long as you don't need any defaults.

Final Thoughts on Generics

That might sound complicated, and it seems to contradict the simplicity of easy-to-use Web Components. But the effort to create a base class is only a one-time task and its usage is a lot easier afterwards.

Figure 2-6 shows the example with a typed base interface from the type library and additional comments on the property `year`. The editor is now able to help select the right property. That's the main reason for the effort, because in the long term it will increase the code quality.

```
class TimeProperties implements Intl.DateTimeFormatOptions {
  datetime: string = '';
  /**
   * How to show the year (2020 or 20)
   */
  year: 'numeric' | '2-digit' = 'numeric';
  month: 'numeric' | '2-digit' | 'narrow' | 'short' | 'long' = 'numeric';
  day: 'numeric' | '2-digit' = 'numeric';
  hour: 'numeric' | '2-digit' = 'numeric';
  minute: 'numeric' | '2-digit' = 'numeric';
  second: 'numeric' | '2-digit' = 'numeric';
  timeZoneName: 'short' | 'long' = 'short';
}

@Observes(TimeProperties)
class TimeFormat extends BaseComponent<TimeProperties> {

  constructor() {
    super();
  }

  render() { // (1)
    let date = new Date(this.data.datetime || Date.now());

    this.innerHTML = new Intl.DateTimeFormat("default", {
      year: this.data.year || undefined,
      month: this.data      datetime
      day: this.data.d      day
      hour: this.data.      hour
      minute: this.dat      minute
      second: this.dat      month
      timeZoneName: th      second
    }).format(date);       timeZoneName
  }                        year
```

(property) TimeProperties.year: "numeric" | "2-digit"

How to show the year (2020 or 20)

Figure 2-6. *Real-life example with IntelliSense*

Summary

In this chapter, I covered the basics of Web Components, the ways to create one, enhance it, and work with it in abstract and real-life code examples. Furthermore, the API to change the component's behavior was explained, as was how to interact with such components by observing attribute changes and firing events.

CHAPTER 3

Shadow DOM

The Shadow DOM brings encapsulation. It allows a component to have its very own DOM tree, which can't be accidentally accessed from the main document, may have local style rules, and more. When creating a new component, the component's developer doesn't need to know anything about the application this particular component is running in. That further simplifies the development.

In older literature, you may find the elements `<shadow>` and `<content>`. Both are deprecated and no longer part of the current Web Component standard.

Preparation

To recap some of the facts shown here, it's recommended to have the Chrome browser available. To deal with the Shadow DOM, just activate the appropriate feature (see Figure 3-1) in Dev Tools settings (F12) and you're good to go. The settings are available through the cog icon in the upper right corner of the Developers Tools page.

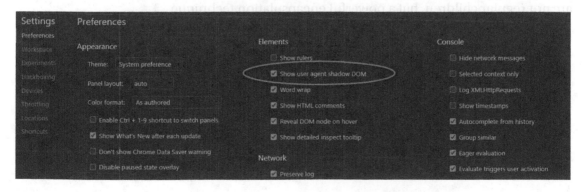

Figure 3-1. *Activating the Shadow DOM for debugging in Chrome*

J. Krause, *Developing Web Components with TypeScript*, https://doi.org/10.1007/978-1-4842-6840-7_3

Of course, other browsers support this feature too, but the settings might be different.

Built-in Shadow DOM

Complex browser controls are created and styled internally in different ways. Let's have a look into `<input type="range">` as an example. The browser uses DOM/CSS internally to draw them. That DOM structure is normally hidden from the developer, but you can see it in the developer tools with the Shadow DOM option enabled, as mentioned.

The `<input type="range">` can be seen in Chrome's dev tools, as shown in Figure 3-2.

Figure 3-2. *A natural Shadow DOM in Chrome's dev tools*

What you see under `#shadow-root` is called a Shadow DOM. It's a piece of completely isolated code, made with the standard techniques like HTML and CSS. You can't get built-in Shadow DOM elements by regular JavaScript calls or selectors. These are not regular children, but a powerful encapsulation technique.

In the example above, you can see a useful attribute named `webkit-slider-runnable-track`. It's non-standard; in fact, it exists for historical reasons. You can use it to style subelements with CSS like this:

```
<style>
/* make the slider track red */
input::-webkit-slider-runnable-track {
  background: red;
}
</style>

<input type="range">
```

Once again, this is a non-standard attribute. It's specific to browsers using the Chromium engine. But a similar structure can be expected in all other engines, and sometimes it helps to achieve weird requirements.

Here, it's just a primer to show that there is more under the hood. The Shadow DOM of a Web Component is a way to work with encapsulation in a well-defined way.

Shadow Tree

A DOM element can have two types of DOM sub-trees:

- **Light tree**: A regular DOM sub-tree, made of HTML children. All sub-trees that you saw so far were "light."

- **Shadow tree**: A hidden DOM sub-tree, not reflected in HTML, hidden from users' eyes.

If an element has both, then the browser renders only the shadow tree. But you can set up a kind of composition between shadow and light trees as well. More details are explained in Chapter 6.

Terms

There are a few terms here you should know:

- **Shadow host**: The host component

- **Shadow root**: The root of the partial tree that forms the shadow tree

- **Shadow DOM**: An isolated DOM that contains the content of the tree

- **Shadow boundary**: The border around the whole thing, including the root and tree

The relations between these parts are shown in Figure 3-3.

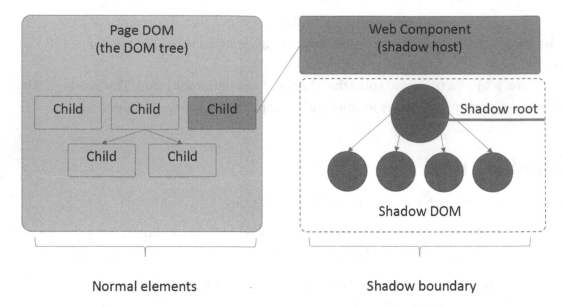

Figure 3-3. *Page DOM and Shadow DOM*

The access to the inner DOM is the same as for the regular DOM, which means you can use the same methods to manipulate the content. The methods might return different values and access different parts of the page (or nothing at all), though.

Using Shadow Trees

The shadow tree can be used in custom elements to hide component internals and apply component-local styles. For example, this <show-hello> element hides its internal DOM in a shadow tree:

```
<script>
customElements.define('show-hello', class extends HTMLElement {
  connectedCallback() {
    const shadow = this.attachShadow({mode: 'open'});
    shadow.innerHTML = `<p>
      Hello, ${this.getAttribute('name')}
    </p>`;
  }
});
</script>
<show-hello name="Joerg"></show-hello>
```

Figure 3-4 shows how the resulting DOM looks in the Chrome dev tools. All of the content is placed under the #shadow-root (open) tag.

```
▼<body>
  ▼<show-hello name="Joerg">
    ▼#shadow-root (open)
        <p>
                   Hello, Joerg
           </p> == $0
    </show-hello>
  </body>
</html>
```

Figure 3-4. *Appearance in the Chrome dev tools*

The call to this.attachShadow({mode: ...}) creates a shadow tree. The options are open and closed. I'll explain this shortly.

Limitations

There are some limitations you must consider:

- You can create only one shadow root per component.

- The component must be either a custom element or derive from one of these:

  - <article>, represented through the API class HTMLArticleElement

  - <aside>, represented through the API class HTMLAsideElement

  - <blockquote>, represented through the API class HTMLBlockquoteElement

  - <body>, represented through the API class HTMLBodyElement

  - <div>, represented through the API class HTMLDivElement

  - <footer>, represented through the API class HTMLFooterElement

  - <h1...h6>, represented through the API class HTMLHeadElement

  - <header>, represented through the API class HTMLHeaderElement

47

- `<main>`, represented through the API class `HTMLMainElement`

- `<nav>`, represented through the API class `HTMLNavElement`

- `<p>`, represented through the API class `HTMLParagraphElement`

- `<section>`, represented through the API class `HTMLSectionElement`

- `<span>`, represented through the API class `HTMLSpanElement`

Other elements, like `<img>`, can't host a shadow tree. The basic rule is that the element must be able to host some content at all. That means it must make sense to add something within. That's the case for all containers such as `<span>`, but not `<img>`, which is "just there" but has an image in it, nothing else one could add.

Modes

The mode option sets the encapsulation level. It must have one of two values:

- open: The shadow root is available as `this.shadowRoot`. Any code (JavaScript) is able to access the shadow tree of the element.

- closed: `this.shadowRoot` is always null, and there is no access through code (sort of total isolation).

You can only access the Shadow DOM by the reference returned by `attachShadow` (and probably hidden inside a class). Browser-native shadow trees, such as `<input type="range">`, are closed. There's no way to access them.

The shadow root, returned by `attachShadow`, is like an element. You can use `innerHTML` or DOM methods, such as `append`, to populate it. In fact, the @nyaf thin library code uses `innerHTML` to assign the rendered content to the Web Component. It's as simple as it sounds.

The element with a shadow root is called a *shadow tree host* and is available as the shadow root `host` property. This will work only in open mode:

```
var hostElement = elem.shadowRoot.host;
```

If you use this in a base class, it's easy and powerful to copy data from host to shadow and back.

Encapsulation

The Shadow DOM is strongly delimited from the main document. Shadow DOM elements are not visible to querySelector from the light DOM. In particular, Shadow DOM elements may have identifiers that conflict with those in the light DOM. They must be unique only within the shadow tree. Also, the Shadow DOM has its own stylesheets. Style rules from the outer DOM don't get applied, at least not directly. There are pseudo classes that help here to apply externally provided styles. You can find more about this in Chapter 7.

An example shows how it works directly. First, a global style is created:

```
<style>
  p { color: red; }
</style>
Imagine a document, that contains that style and a web component definition:

<div id="elem"></div>

<script>
  const elem = this.querySelector('#elem');
  elem.attachShadow({mode: 'open'});
  elem.shadowRoot.innerHTML = `
    <style> p { font-weight: bold; } </style>
    <p>Hello, Joerg!</p>
  `;
  console.log(document.querySelectorAll('p').length);
  console.log(elem.shadowRoot.querySelectorAll('p').length);
</script>
```

Three effects can be recognized here:

- The style from the document does not affect the shadow tree. The color is not red.

- The style from the inside works. The element is bold.

- To get elements in a shadow tree, you must query from inside the tree (elem.shadowRoot).

In the example, I use `length` to check for elements. If there is nothing, the value is 0 and at runtime JavaScript treats this as `false`.

A bit more verbose code might be better readable. If you write library code, stay with the shortest option available; for business code, the verbose variant is usually better.

Shadow DOM without Components

Just as a sidestep, it's worth to mention that using Web Components is not a condition for using the Shadow DOM. You can create a Shadow DOM on the fly without using Web Components. Assume this regular HTML element:

```
<div id="shadowHost"></div>
```

Add some code to see how it creates the Shadow DOM:

```
const shadow = document.querySelector('#shadowHost').createShadowRoot();
shadow.innerHTML = `
  <p>Some text in the element.</p>
  <style>p { color: red; border: 1px dashed; }</style>
`;
```

You now have an existing element upgraded with a piece of isolated DOM and some content hidden from the rest of page (see Figure 3-5).

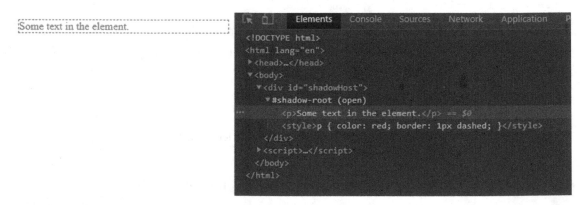

Figure 3-5. *Quick creation of a Shadow DOM*

Closing the Shadow Root

In all previous examples and in most examples in this book, I use the open mode to attach a shadow root. If you really do not need access to the root and have nothing to apply programmatically, consider closing the root by using closed.

```
const shadowroot = element.attachShadow({ mode: 'closed' });
```

In this case, the element.shadowRoot returns null and obviously you can do nothing with it.

The Shadow Root API

The ShadowRoot interface of the Shadow DOM API is the root node of a DOM subtree that is rendered separately from a document's main DOM tree. This is what you get with element.shadowRoot.

Properties

Some properties give access to the internal parts of a component:

- delegatesFocus: A read-only property that returns a boolean that indicates whether delegatesFocus was set when the shadow was attached

- host: A read-only property that returns a reference to the DOM element the shadow root is attached to

- innerHTML: Sets or returns a reference to the DOM tree inside the shadow root

- mode: A read-only property that returns the mode of the shadow root, either open or closed. This defines whether or not the shadow root's internal features are accessible from JavaScript.

The ShadowRoot interface includes the following properties defined on the DocumentOrShadowRoot mixin. Note that this is currently only implemented by Chrome. Other browsers make this available in the Document.

- `activeElement`: A read-only property that returns the `Element` within the shadow tree that has focus

- `styleSheets`: A read-only property that returns a `StyleSheetList` of `CSSStyleSheet` objects for stylesheets explicitly linked into or embedded in a document

Methods

Some methods extend this API:

- `getSelection()`: A method that returns a `Selection` object representing the range of text selected by the user or the current position of the caret

- `elementFromPoint()`: A method that returns the topmost element at the specified coordinates

- `elementsFromPoint()`: A method that returns an array of all elements at the specified coordinates

- `caretPositionFromPoint()`: A method that returns a `CaretPosition` object containing the DOM node containing the caret and caret's character offset within that node (the caret is the blinking point where the user starts typing)

Similar incompatibilities, like for the properties, appear when accessing these methods. This depends on the browser version and manufacturer. Because the situation changes with each new version, it's hard to give clear advice here. The best bet is to first define what browsers and versions you need to support. Then have a look on MDN (Mozilla Developer Network) for any support issues and seek a polyfill to help solve compatibility issues.

Summary

In this chapter, I covered the Shadow DOM, the isolated inner part of a Web Component. Several API calls are available to deal with the Shadow DOM and its root element. You can also find examples of how the Shadow DOM looks in a browser's development tool.

CHAPTER 4

Events

The idea behind the shadow tree is to encapsulate internal implementation details of a component. This requires exposing events explicitly if you still want to interact with the inner parts of a component.

Let's say a click event happens inside a Shadow DOM of the `<user-card>` component. But scripts in the main document have no idea about the Shadow DOM internals. So, to keep the details encapsulated, the browser has to retarget the event. Events that happen in the Shadow DOM have the host element as the target when caught outside of the component.

Events in ECMAScript

Before you deal with custom events, you should have a basic understanding of the event schema in JavaScript. To learn more, I recommend having a look at the Mozilla Developer Network (MDN) at `https://developer.mozilla.org`.

Event Handlers

On the occurrence of an event, the application executes a set of related tasks. The block of code that achieves this purpose is called the *event handler*. Every HTML element has a set of events associated with it. You can define how the events will be processed in JavaScript by using event handlers. Sometimes the handler appears as a callback, a function that's provided as a parameter. You can read the callback as the technical solution to create an event handler.

© Jörg Krause 2021
J. Krause, *Developing Web Components with TypeScript*, https://doi.org/10.1007/978-1-4842-6840-7_4

Assigning a Handler

To assign a handler, you have two options. The first is an attribute on the HTML element. In this case, the name starts with an on. For instance, the click event is called onclick. Second, you can attach an event to an element object using the HTML 5 API. In this case, the pure name is used, so click remains click. Because you code Web Components and deal with them as objects, you will usually use the second method exclusively. There is also a combination of both methods possible, where you assign the handler function to an event property. And these event properties are the same as the attribute (with an on prefix).

```
<button onclick="sendData()">Send Data</button>
const button = this.querySelector('button');
button.addEventListener('click', e => sendData(e));
const button = this.querySelector('button');
button.onclick = sendData;
```

Choosing the Right Events

While the handling is not that difficult, choosing the right event is much harder. Of course, just using click sounds easy. But the sheer number of events is frightening.

HTML 5 Standard Events

The standard HTML 5 events are well defined and can be found at several sources online. I recommend having a look at https://developer.mozilla.org/en-US/docs/Web/Events and, because it's a bit overwhelming, especially the "Standard Events" section on that page.

Event Bubbling

Event bubbling is a strange term but nonetheless it is very important. You can view an HTML page as a stack of layers. Each level of the document tree forms a layer. If you have a document, and within this document is a <div> tag, then the div is on top of the document's body.

A good explanation of this technique can be found among the standard descriptions provided by W3C (World Wide Web Consortium) at www.w3.org/TR/ DOM-Level-3-Events/#event-flow.

Then the lower layer is body and the upper layer is div. This three-dimensional view of the otherwise flat document is helpful for understanding event handling. Assume that the user clicks with the mouse onto the div element. We'll skip the operating system stuff here and capture only the events already assigned to the browser's window.

To get the bubbling right, it's important to understand that the mouse event comes from the top. So it hits the div first. If there is a handler attached, it can be handled. Otherwise, the event is forwarded to the next layer, which in this example is the document itself. This is called *bubbling*, because it looks like bubbles in a bottle moving upwards until they hit something and crash. In the browser, the bubbling goes even further:

```
Target -> Body -> HTML -> Document -> Window
```

If you have many elements on the page that form a deep hierarchy, then the bubbles have a long way through all of them. But this behavior is something you can control. The way upwards is technically called *propagation*. In the API of the event handler you get an event object. This object can be used to change the behavior by calling the stopPropagation method as shown here:

```
div.addEventListener("click", event => {
  event.stopPropagation();
});
```

The Event Object

The event object provides a lot of information about the event. For example, the mouse events deliver the clicked mouse button and coordinates. The key events will obviously provide the actual key the user hit. Among these simple properties there are a few subtle ones.

Because the propagation may let the event bubble, it's not entirely clear whether you are on the target directly or somewhere up the chain. That's the reason you can capture the actual element using event.target. That's the element that received the click or whatever. But the handler could be somewhere up (in the direction of the document). This element is delivered using `event.currentTarget`. Imagine a list, (`<ul><li></ul>`). Instead of attaching a handler to each list item, it's much easier to just attach one to the whole list (ul). If the user clicks an item, the `target` is the `li` element, while `currentTarget` is ul (though quite often both properties deliver the same element).

Be aware that even if almost all events bubble, not all do so. Sometimes it doesn't make sense. One popular example is `focus`. It's fired if an input element, such as a text box, receives the cursor. Input elements are never nested, so there is no way to handle a focus somewhere in the chain. In that case, the event is either handled or dropped.

After the bubbling phase, the capturing phase starts. This means each element on the bubble way will be informed that the event has been handled.

Stopping Other Handlers

If an element has multiple event handlers on a single event, then even if one of them stops the bubbling, the other ones will still execute. In other words, `event.stopPropagation` stops the move upwards, but on the current element all other handlers will run. To stop the bubbling and prevent handlers on the current element from running, there's the method `event.stopImmediatePropagation`. After it no other handlers execute.

Other Types of Propagation

Event capturing is another type of event propagation. It is basically the way back to the event's source.

Event Capturing

To turn event capturing on, pass `true` as the third argument to the `addEventListener` method:

```
Element.addEventListener("click", function(){}, true);
```

This type of propagation is rarely used. Instead of working from inner to outer, it flips the direction and goes from outer to inner. Here is the hierarchy:

```
Window -> Document -> HTML -> Body -> Target
```

Internally the capturing phase precedes the bubbling phase. That's sort of logical, because the operating system has no idea of the internal structure of your document. So it sends the mouse click to the browser window. That's where the capture phase starts, silently and in the background until it hits an element that has a handler attached. Then the bubbling phase begins. That's where you get aware of the event and start dealing with it.

Removing Handlers

To remove a handler, just call `event.removeEventListener` with the same parameters you used to add it. This can be done only in code. There is no way to remove a handler added in markup.

Multiple Handlers

You can attach multiple handlers and they will execute in the order you assign them. This can be done only in code. There is no way to add more than one handler in markup.

Stopping Default Behavior

Several elements react to events out of the box. For example, an anchor element will follow the `href` attribute on a mouse click. If you attach a handler, this private handler will execute first, but the internal behavior will happen afterwards. That can be very annoying if you have the handler to prevent this. To suppress this behavior, you call a method named `preventDefault()`. You may have seen returning `false` from the event handler to achieve the same. But that's an exception and is designed to support this behavior with the *on[event]* syntax. A handler attached directly in HTML doesn't receive an event object. Without that, you wouldn't be able to prevent anything. But, you can return `false` as a solution. In all other situations, the return value is ignored.

You may very often see event handlers that use both `preventDefault` and `return false`. Apart from the exception described before, this is plain wrong.

Follow-Up Events

Some events form chains. Let's take `keypress` as an example. It's a full key cycle. But before this event comes, you can receive a `keydown` and a `keyup`. A similar thing happens for `click`, which starts with `mousedown` and is followed by `mouseup`. It's important for the infrastructure to work that way because the information is needed to detect, for example, a `dblclick`.

Passive Events

The optional `passive: true` option of `addEventListener` signals to the browser that the handler is not going to call `preventDefault()`. This is needed because there are some events like `touchmove` on mobile devices (when the user moves their finger across the screen) that cause scrolling by default, but that scrolling can be prevented using `preventDefault()`. When the browser detects such an event, it first must process all handlers, and then if `preventDefault` is not called anywhere, it can proceed with scrolling. This may cause unnecessary delays in the UI. The option tells the browser that the handler is not going to cancel scrolling. Then the browser scrolls, immediately providing a maximally fluent experience, and the event is handled later on. Passive is `true` by default for `touchstart` and `touchmove` on most browsers.

Document Handlers

It's quite often a good idea (and sometimes it makes your life really easy) to stop thinking about adding endless chains of handlers to a growing number of elements. Because the event bubbles anyway, it's a good solution to add a few handlers (mouse, key, submit) to the document and just check the `e.target` property whether you got the right one. A clever approach is to use the `dataSet` property, reflected in HTML as `data-` attributes. Say you want a button click to handle something using a global handler. See the code in Listing 4-1.

Listing 4-1. Document Events (chapter4/docs/index.html)

```
<button data-form-id="subscribe-mail" data-action-id="submit">
  Show Mail Form
</button>
<form id="subscribe-mail" hidden>
  Your mail: <input type="email">
</form>
<script>
  document.addEventListener('click', function(event) {
    let id = event.target.dataset.formId;
    if (!id) return;
    let elem = document.getElementById(id);
    elem.hidden = !elem.hidden;
    let action = event.target.dataset.actionId;
    if (action) {
      // add logic to submit the form
    }
  });
</script>
```

The event in this example is added to the document. Because it's the underlying layer, it will receive all unhandled and propagated events. With just one handler you can handle all events globally. This can help you write code that's easier to maintain.

Events in Web Components

Listing 4-2 shows a simple example with an event handler attached on the Shadow DOM.

Listing 4-2. Component Events (chapter4/comp/index.html)

```
<user-card></user-card>

<script>
customElements.define('user-card', class extends HTMLElement {
  connectedCallback() {
    this.attachShadow({mode: 'open'});
```

```
    this.shadowRoot.innerHTML = `<p>
      <button>Click me</button>
    </p>`;
    this.shadowRoot.firstElementChild.onclick =
      e => alert("Inner target: " + e.target.tagName);
  }
});

document.onclick =
  e => alert("Outer target: " + e.target.tagName);
</script>
```

If you click on the button, the messages are

- `Inner target: BUTTON` where the internal event handler gets the correct target, the element inside Shadow DOM.

- `Outer target: USER-CARD` where the document event handler gets the shadow host as the target.

Event retargeting is a great thing to have because the outer document doesn't have to know about component internals. From its point of view, the event happened on `<user-card>`.

Events and Slots

Retargeting does not occur if the event occurs on a slotted element that physically lives in the light DOM. In Chapter 6, you can find more details regarding slot behavior. For example, if a user clicks on `<span slot="username">` in the example below, the event target is exactly this *span* element, for both shadow and light handlers (see Listing 4-3).

Listing 4-3. Events and Slots (chapter4/slots/index.html)

```
<user-card id="userCard">
  <span slot="username">Joerg Krause</span>
</user-card>

<script>
customElements.define('user-card', class extends HTMLElement {
```

```
connectedCallback() {
    this.attachShadow({mode: 'open'});
    this.shadowRoot.innerHTML = `<div>
      <b>Name:</b> <slot name="username"></slot>
    </div>`;
    this.shadowRoot.firstElementChild.onclick =
      e => alert("Inner target: " + e.target.tagName);
  }
});
userCard.onclick = e => alert(`Outer target: ${e.target.tagName}`);
</script>
```

If a click happens on "Joerg Krause", for both inner and outer handlers the target is `<span slot="username">`. That's an element from the light DOM, so no retargeting.

On the other hand, if the click occurs on an element originating from the Shadow DOM, such as on `<b>Name:</b>`, then, as it bubbles out of the Shadow DOM, its `event.target` property is reset to `<user-card>`.

Event Bubbling

For purposes of event bubbling, a flattened DOM is used. So, if you have a slotted element and an event occurs somewhere inside it, then it bubbles up to the `<slot>` and upwards.

The full path to the original event target, with all the shadow elements, can be obtained using `event.composedPath()`. As you can see from the name of the method, that path is taken after the composition.

In the example above, the flattened DOM looks like this:

```
<user-card id="userCard">
  #shadow-root
    <div>
      <b>Name:</b>
      <slot name="username">
        <span slot="username">Joerg Krause</span>
      </slot>
    </div>
</user-card>
```

So, for a click on `<span slot="username">`, a call to `event.composedPath()` returns an array:

```
[
  span,
  slot,
  div,
  shadow-root,
  user-card,
  body,
  html,
  document,
  window
]
```

That's exactly the parent chain from the target element in the flattened DOM, after the composition.

Shadow tree details are only provided for {mode: 'open'} trees. If the shadow tree was created with {mode: 'closed'}, then the composed path starts from the host: `user-card` and upwards in the last example.

That's a similar principle as for other methods that work with the Shadow DOM. The internals of closed trees are completely hidden.

Composed Events

Most events successfully bubble through a Shadow DOM boundary. There are few events that do not.

This is governed by the composed event object property. If it's `true`, then the event does cross the boundary. Otherwise, it only can be caught from inside the Shadow DOM.

If you take a look at the UI Events specification, most events have `composed: true`:

- `blur, focus, focusin, focusout`

- `click, dblclick`

- `mousedown, mouseup, mousemove, mouseout, mouseover`

- wheel

- beforeinput, input, keydown, keyup

All touch events and pointer events also have composed: true.
There are some events that have composed: false though:

- mouseenter, mouseleave (they do not bubble at all)

- load, unload, abort, error

- select

- slotchange

These events can be caught only on elements within the same DOM, where the event target resides.

Custom Events

When you dispatch custom events, you need to set both bubbles and composed properties to true for it to bubble up and out of the component.

Synthetic Events

Another name for custom events is *synthetic events*. It's just to distinguish browser internal events.

The code shown in Listing 4-4 creates div#inner in the Shadow DOM of div#outer and triggers two events on it. Only the one with composed: true makes it outside to the document.

Listing 4-4. Custom Events (chapter4/customevent/index.html)

```
<div id="outer"></div>
<script>
outer.attachShadow({mode: 'open'});
let inner = document.createElement('div');
outer.shadowRoot.append(inner);
```

```
document.addEventListener('test', event => alert(event.detail));
inner.dispatchEvent(new CustomEvent('test', {
  bubbles: true,
  composed: true,
  detail: "composed"
}));
inner.dispatchEvent(new CustomEvent('test', {
  bubbles: true,
  composed: false,
  detail: "not composed"
}));
</script>
```

The structure internally looks like this:

```
div(id=outer)
  #shadow-dom
    div(id=inner)
```

This is the view of the content in the browser's developers tools. It shows the Shadow DOM's boundary.

The dispatchEvent API

In the last example, I used the dispatchEvent API. It dispatches an event on a target. The listeners are invoked **synchronously** in their appropriate order. The normal event processing rules apply. An outside viewer can't distinguish between such custom events and those fired by the internal parts of the document. The "event" itself is described by an interface and exists as an instantiable class with the same name. If you work with TypeScript, you have the type and can make instances like this:

```
const evt = new Event("look", {
  "bubbles":true,
  "cancelable":false
});
document.dispatchEvent(evt);
```

The options dictionary is of type EventInit, with just the three already-mentioned properties:

- bubbles: An optional Boolean indicating whether the event bubbles. The default is false.

- cancelable: An optional Boolean indicating whether the event can be cancelled. The default is false.

- composed: An optional Boolean indicating whether the event will trigger listeners outside of a shadow root. The default is false.

The internal events may fire asynchronously and the internal processing will continue while executing the handlers. This is different with custom events fired by dispatchEvent. This method calls blocks and waits for the handlers to execute. Consider using async techniques if you need a different behavior.

In TypeScript, the definition looks like this:

```
interface EventInit {
    bubbles?: boolean;
    cancelable?: boolean;
    composed?: boolean;
}

interface Event {
    readonly bubbles: boolean;
    cancelBubble: boolean;
    readonly cancelable: boolean;
    readonly composed: boolean;
    readonly currentTarget: EventTarget | null;
    readonly defaultPrevented: boolean;
    readonly eventPhase: number;
    readonly isTrusted: boolean;
    returnValue: boolean;
    /** deprecated (only for old browsers) */
    readonly srcElement: EventTarget | null;
    readonly target: EventTarget | null;
```

```
    readonly timeStamp: number;
    readonly type: string;
    composedPath(): EventTarget[];
    initEvent(
      type: string,
      bubbles?: boolean,
      cancelable?: boolean): void;
    preventDefault(): void;
    stopImmediatePropagation(): void;
    stopPropagation(): void;
    readonly AT_TARGET: number;
    readonly BUBBLING_PHASE: number;
    readonly CAPTURING_PHASE: number;
    readonly NONE: number;
}

declare var Event: {
    prototype: Event;
    new(type: string, eventInitDict?: EventInit): Event;
    readonly AT_TARGET: number;
    readonly BUBBLING_PHASE: number;
    readonly CAPTURING_PHASE: number;
    readonly NONE: number;
};
```

Customize Events

Apart from the common Event interface, there is another type you can use: CustomEvent. Despite the name, you don't need to use it to fire a custom event, but it's often helpful to get clearer information about the nature of the event. The only difference is that CustomEvent provides an additional property called detail. This is an object you define on the source and the receiver can get custom data here. The sheer existence clarifies the custom nature of the event. The option is part of the initializer, now named CustomEventInit.

```
// this.process omitted for brevity
obj.addEventListener("loop", (e) => { this.process(e.detail) });

// create and dispatch the event
var event = new CustomEvent("loop", {
  detail: {
    loops: 100
  }
});
obj.dispatchEvent(event);
```

The CustomEventInit type accepts all properties from EventInit, too.
In TypeScript, the definition looks like this:

```
interface CustomEventInit<T = any> extends EventInit {
    detail?: T;
}

interface CustomEvent<T = any> extends Event {
    readonly detail: T;
    initCustomEvent(
      typeArg: string,
      canBubbleArg: boolean,
      cancelableArg: boolean,
      detailArg: T): void;
}

declare var CustomEvent: {
    prototype: CustomEvent;
    new<T>(
      typeArg: string,
      eventInitDict?: CustomEventInit<T>): CustomEvent<T>;
};
```

This provides both a type definition and a constructor description.

Smart Events

Adding events requires script work. To make it easier to use, some global code can be helpful. However, this doesn't change the basic behavior and flow as described before. Events are defined by a special instruction. They are attached to document objects, regardless of usage.

Events are easy to add directly using a dataset like data-onclick. All JavaScript events are supported this way. Just replace onclick in the example with any other JavaScript event:

```
<button data-on-click="clickId">OK</button>
```

Now, on an applications global start script (see Listing 4-5), attach handlers to anything with such an event definition.

Listing 4-5. Smart Events (chapter4/smart/index.html)

```
document.querySelectorAll('[^data-on-]').forEach(elem => {
  const events = elem.dataSet.filter(d => d.startsWidth('on'));
  events.forEach(event =>  {
    elem.addEventHandler(event, e => {
      // global handler
      const instruction = e.target.dataSet(event);
      // deal with it
    });
  });
});
```

The effect here is, depending on the number of such events, to drastically reduce the amount of code for attaching events. However, it's not that easy to add similar removeEventHandler calls. The code is more appropriate for a single-page app, where the final state of the code is static and held in memory anyway.

Summary

In this chapter, I explained event handling in the browser, the way to attach events to normal and shadowed Web Components and how to extend the event system. By using custom events, the way components communicate to each other can be easily extended. Some TypeScript definitions show how the objects are built internally. Attaching events globally using the `document` object shows how to minimize the effort to attach multiple events.

CHAPTER 5

Templates

The concept of templates is a fundamental part of almost all web development environments. Examples for server-side template languages are Razor (.NET), Haml (Ruby), Django (Python), Pug (NodeJS), and Smarty (PHP). Examples for client-side template languages can be found in Angular and many more frameworks.

Templates help create dynamic parts, reduce boilerplate code, and avoid repeating markup. The rise of so many template variants in web frameworks, client- and server-side, was forced by a missing alternative in HTML. That changed dramatically with the WhatWG HTML Template Specification. HTML templates still struggle to be widely accepted, but with usage in Web Components they find their way back into the light.

HTML 5 Templates

A built-in `<template>` element serves as storage for HTML markup templates. The browser ignores its contents and only checks for syntax validity, but you can access and use it in JavaScript to create or enhance other elements. All modern browsers support this, but to ensure it's really fully supported you may consider a small test:

```
function hasTemplateSupport() {
  return 'content' in document.createElement('template');
}
if (hasTemplateSupport()) {
  // Use it
} else {
  // Fall back to a library
}
```

© Jörg Krause 2021
J. Krause, *Developing Web Components with TypeScript*, https://doi.org/10.1007/978-1-4842-6840-7_5

How It Works

In theory, you could create any invisible element somewhere in HTML to store some HTML markup for using later in scripts. The special thing about ‹template› is the nature of being cloneable. The content can be any valid HTML. This includes fragments of code that would be invalid if just written on their own.

For example, you can put a table row ‹tr› in the template and as a fragment it's valid:

```
<template>
  <tr>
    <td>Contents</td>
  </tr>
</template>
```

Usually, if you try to put ‹tr› inside, say, a ‹div›, the browser detects this as an invalid DOM structure and tries to "fix" it by adding a ‹table› around it. That's not what you want. The ‹template› element keeps its content exactly like you wrote it there.

You can put styles and scripts into ‹template› as well:

```
<template>
  <style>
    p { font-weight: bold; }
  </style>
  <script>
    alert("Hello");
  </script>
</template>
```

The browser considers ‹template› content "out of the document." Hence, styles are not applied, scripts are not executed, the autoplay of a video element is not run, and much more. Technically, it's inert until activated. The content becomes live (styles applied, scripts run, and so on) when it's being inserted into the document. Also, if you try to access it from outside, using querySelector or other API calls, these functions will not see the template's content.

You may ask where to place the <template> element if it isn't part of the document anyway. The answer is: It doesn't matter. It may appear in the <head> element or somewhere in the body among other elements. Its location depends on the actual content, so put it where it makes more sense. Global templates may be better placed in the head, while a row template for some tables is probably easier to handle within the table itself. It's a question of coding style, not a technical requirement.

Activating a Template

The template content is available in its content property as a DocumentFragment, which is a special type of DOM node. You can treat it as any other DOM node, except one special property. You don't insert the template itself, but instead its children, available through the property content. The example in Listing 5-1 shows how to use it.

Listing 5-1. Simple Template (chapter5/template/index.html)

```
<template id="tmpl">
  <script>
    alert("Hello");
  </script>
  <div class="message">Hello, template!</div>
</template>

<script>
  let elem = document.createElement('div');
  elem.append(tmpl.content.cloneNode(true));
  document.body.append(elem);
</script>
```

The interesting part here is that you don't need to select the template. Based on its id property, it's already available as a global property. This means tmpl.content is available after the browser has parsed the document and there is no need to query the element explicitly. If you query (document.querySelector('#tmpl')), the result would be exactly the same. The result is shown in Figure 5-1.

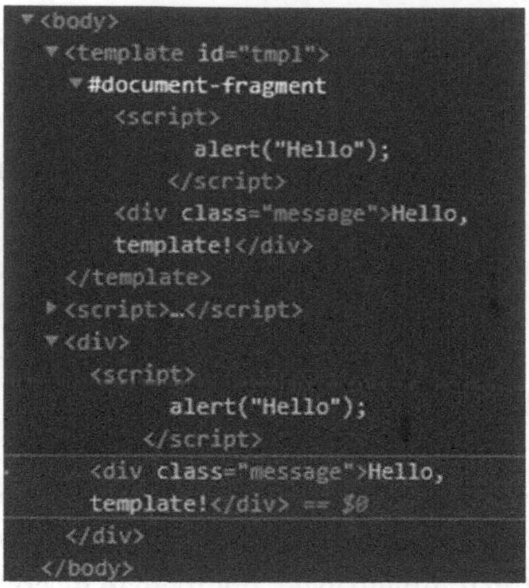

Figure 5-1. *Appearance of the template and clone in the DOM*

Clone or Import

There are several methods to clone or import nodes. You need a deep copy, but apart from this it's really up to you. One method is `importNode` and the other is `cloneNode`. Historically, the `importNode` method was made to copy content from one document to the other. You may see the template with its document fragment as such a node source and the actual document as the node sink. But technically it's a clone operation and here the `cloneNode` method seems more appropriate. However, it's academic because both methods lead to *exactly* the same result. Modern browsers don't distinguish here anymore in relation to templates. However, if you read out the `ownerDocument` property, it could have a different value when using `importNode`. Let's rewrite the last example to show the difference; see Listing 5-2.

Listing 5-2. Simple Template (chapter5/importnode/index.html)

```
<template id="tmpl">
  <script>
    alert("Hello");
  </script>
  <div class="message">Hello, template!</div>
</template>
```

```
<script>
  let elem = document.createElement('div');
  elem.append(document.importNode(tmpl.content, true));
  document.body.append(elem);
</script>
```

Personally, I find the cloneNode way more intuitive and easier to read. But it may depend on the real code whether other options suit better.

Don't forget to clone the node! Otherwise the template's content will be moved on the first attempt and further access will hit an empty template.

Templates and Web Components

Templates play a crucial role in Web Components. They are a fundamental part of creating powerful components. The main purpose is to handle the Shadow DOM properly, either as part of a component or somewhere directly in the DOM.

Shadow DOM

Let's create a Shadow DOM example using the <template> element. See Listing 5-3.

Listing 5-3. Template with Shadow DOM (chapter5/shadow/index.html)

```
<template id="tmpl">
  <style> p { font-weight: bold; } </style>
  <p id="message"></p>
</template>

<div id="elem">Click me</div>

<script>
  elem.onclick = function() {
    elem.attachShadow({mode: 'open'});
    elem.shadowRoot.append(tmpl.content.cloneNode(true));
    elem.shadowRoot.getElementById('message').innerHTML = "Hello Shadow!";
  };
</script>
```

Figure 5-2 shows the result in the browser's developers tools.

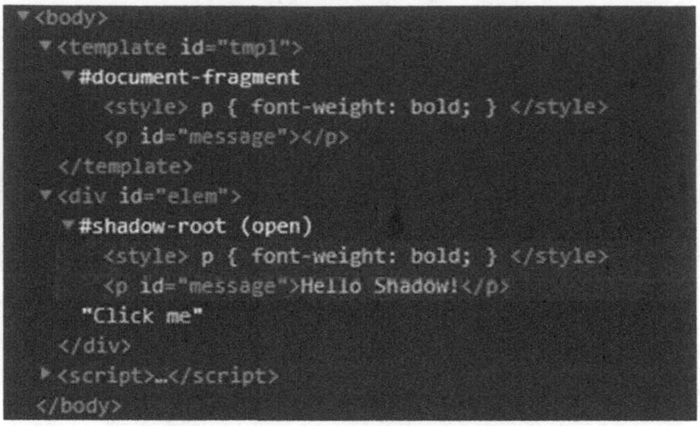

Figure 5-2. *Isolating template content in a shadow root*

In line 10 when you clone and insert `tmpl.content`, instead of the `DocumentFragment` the template is made off, its children `<style>` and `<p>` are inserted. They form the Shadow DOM, then.

Using createShadowRoot

You may have seen examples using `createShadowRoot` to create the shadow root. It's a deprecated method and should not be used any longer, even though it is still reliably available in all major browsers.

Shadow DOM and innerHTML

After the initial decision to use the Shadow DOM, the next question is how to get content in there. If the template isn't your concern, you may end up with something like Listing 5-4.

Listing 5-4. Shadow with innerHTML (chapter5/inner/index.html)

```
<div id="host"></div>
<script>
  var elem = document.querySelector('#host');
  elem.attachShadow({ mode: 'open' });
  elem.shadowRoot.innerHTML = '<span>Host node</span>';
</script>
```

That's fine for smaller examples. But using string for HTML is a way to mess up things for sure. If you can't switch to a template engine such as JSX or import the HTML from documents, using the `<template>` element is the better way to go. See Listing 5-5.

Listing 5-5. Simple Template (chapter5/innertemplate/index.html)

```
<div id="host"></div>
<template id="tmpl">
  <span>Host node</span>
</template>
<script>
  var elem = document.querySelector('#host');
  elem.attachShadow({ mode: 'open' });
  elem.shadowRoot.appendChild(tmpl.content.cloneNode(true));
</script>
```

Nested Templates

Consider the example in Listing 5-6 with a template inside another template.

Listing 5-6. Nested Templates (chapter5/nested/index.html)

```
<template id="section">
  <h1>Header</h1>
  <p>Text</p>
  <template id="details">
    <h1>Addition</h1>
    <p>Details</p>
  </template>
</template>
```

While this is allowed, the activation is not so simple. The inner template remains inert even if the outer is properly activated. You need to activate both separately. That's not a big effort but it's tricky in all the details. See Listing 5-7.

Listing 5-7. Nested Templates, cont. (chapter5/nested/index.html)

```
const elem = document.querySelector('#host');
const outer = section.content.cloneNode(true);
const inner = outer.children.details;
outer.removeChild(inner);
outer.appendChild(inner.content.cloneNode(true));
elem.appendChild(outer);
```

Whether you work with or without Shadow DOM doesn't matter. For the sake of clarity, the example in Listing 5-7 goes straight. First, the outer template is pulled using the magic property `section` that corresponds to the templates `id` property (line 2). Then it's cloned. The clone has a collection of children and among them is the inner template. Even here you can use the magic property called `details` according to the inner template's `id` (line 3). Because the deep clone with `cloneNode` will also clone the inner template, you remove it (line 4). It's not really disturbing anything but we love clean code. Hence, you clone the inner part, add it to the outer clone (line 5), and attach the whole construct to the real DOM (line 6). See Figure 5-3.

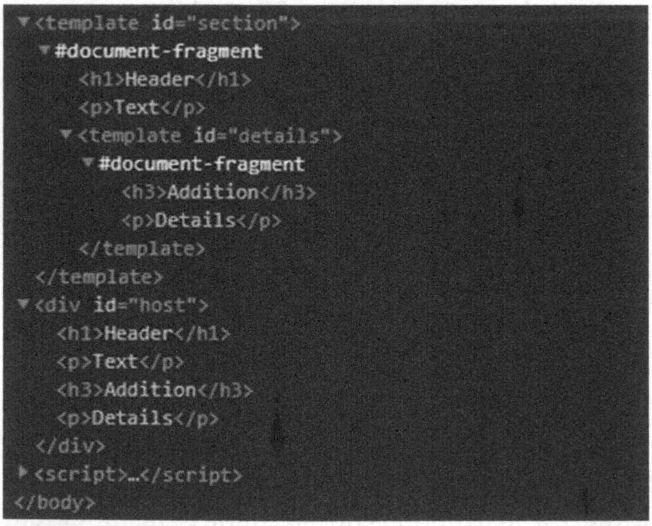

Figure 5-3. *Nested templates in the debug view*

Making inner templates invisible to the first layer allows you to keep the template structure clean and readable.

Template Styles

Styles in templates behave like any other style. A style node can be copied like any other node. But you can also access the host element by using the pseudo selector :host. More about this can be found in Chapter 7.

Applying Global Styles

The following example takes care of the template behavior. It uses the template element if needed to create a Shadow DOM. It's the regular creation of a shadowed Web Component using a separate method. It's not complete for the sake of brevity, but it shows the idea. Just call this method in the constructor of a Web Component. The code assumes you have static property named withShadow that's either present or not. It could be defined on the component definition to make it available on all instances. The constructor call is placed in a base class to make it available to all components.

```
setup() {
  if (    this.constructor    .withShadow) {
    const template = document.createElement('template');
    template.innerHTML = this.render();
    if (!this.shadowRoot || this.shadowRoot.mode === 'closed') {
      this.attachShadow({ mode: 'open' });
      // copy styles to shadow if shadowed and there is something to add
      if (this.copyStyles) {
        const style = document.createElement('style');
        style.textContent = this.globalStyles;
        this.shadowRoot.appendChild(style);
      }
      this.shadowRoot.appendChild(template.content.cloneNode(true));
    }
  } else {
    this.innerHTML = this.render();
  }
}
```

The property this.copyStyles provides a Boolean value to control the behavior. Assume it's an observed attribute to control a component's behavior from the usage side. If it's true, the setup code creates a style element and copies some prepared styles into it. This works even with plain text. The property this.globalStyles is this source. Either it's provided as an attribute or you set up some code in the Web Components constructor to copy all global styles in one step. This would bring both isolation and global style access. It's not always the ideal solution, but it's often a quick win for complex CSS frameworks.

Copying global styles could look like this:

```
for (let i = 0; i < this.ownerDocument.styleSheets.length; i++) {
  const css = this.ownerDocument.styleSheets[i] as CSSStyleSheet;
  try {
    if (!css.rules || css.rules.length === 0) {
      continue;
    }
    this.globalStyles += Object.keys(css.cssRules)
      .map(k => css.cssRules[k].cssText ?? ' ')
      .join(' ');
  } catch(err) {
    console.warn(err);
  }
}
```

Place this code in the component's constructor. If you do this for multiple documents, consider making the property this.globalStyles static, check for already copied styles, and skip the code if it's already there. Then the first component enhanced in such a way pulls the styles and all others in your document benefit silently.

The thin library documented in the Appendix contains such a solution, and you can look for a complete example in the sources. It's in the class BaseComponent.

Summary

In this chapter, you learned about templates and how you can use them with or without Web Components. I also explained the usage of templates with slots, nested templates, and how to deal with styles.

CHAPTER 6

Slots

A slot is a placeholder that users can fill with their own markup. The slot may exist
outside a Web Component or inside, in conjunction with a template or a Shadow DOM
(or both).

Slots Explained

Many types of components, such as tabs, menus, image galleries, and so on, need
dynamic content to render properly. Just like a browser's built-in element `<select>`
expects `<option>` items, a `<custom-tabs>` may expect the actual tab content to be
passed. And a `<custom-menu>` may expect menu items.

The code that makes use of `<custom-menu>` could look like this:

```
<custom-menu>
  <title>Languages</title>
  <menu-item>JavaScript</menu-item>
  <menu-item>PHP</menu-item>
  <menu-item>Ruby</menu-item>
</custom-menu>
```

Your component should render it properly as a nice menu with given title and items,
handle menu events, etc.

Slot and Templates

Listing 6-1 shows a shadowed template with some neat styling.

© Jörg Krause 2021
J. Krause, *Developing Web Components with TypeScript*, https://doi.org/10.1007/978-1-4842-6840-7_6

Listing 6-1. Slot Example (chapter6/host/index.html)

```
<template id="tmpl">
  <style>
    :host {
      background: #f8f8f8;
      padding: 10px;
      transition: all 400ms ease-in-out;
      box-sizing: border-box;
      border-radius: 5px;
      width: 450px;
      max-width: 100%;
    }
    :host(:hover) {
      background: #ccc;
    }
    div {
      position: relative;
    }
    header {
      padding: 5px;
      border-bottom: 1px solid #aaa;
    }
    h3 {
      margin: 0 !important;
    }
    textarea {
      font-family: inherit;
      width: 100%;
      height: 100px;
      box-sizing: border-box;
      border: 1px solid #aaa;
    }
```

```
      footer {
        position: absolute;
        bottom: 10px;
        right: 5px;
      }
    </style>
    <div>
      <header>
        <h3>Add a Comment</h3>
      </header>
      <slot name="p"></slot>
      <textarea></textarea>
      <footer>
        <button>Post</button>
      </footer>
    </div>
</template>
<div id="host">
  <p slot="p">Instructions go here</p>
</div>
<script>
  var shadow = document.querySelector('#host');
  shadow.attachShadow({ mode: 'open' });
  shadow.shadowRoot.appendChild(tmpl.content.cloneNode(true));
</script>
```

The idea here is to provide some initial instruction to make the template more dynamic. The slot is some kind of parameter here: <slot name="p"></slot> (line 42).

The name attribute is a reference to the element that has a slot attribute with that name. That's the way to get external information in the template at runtime. The result is shown in Figure 6-1.

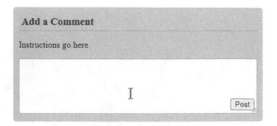

Figure 6-1. *Slot in the browser and debugger*

Shadow DOM

The Shadow DOM supports `<slot>` elements that are automatically filled by the content from the light DOM. The above example is already "shadowed," but that's just an option. There is no need for the slots to use a Shadow DOM.

Slots and Components

Let's see how slots work on a simple example with Web Components. Listing 6-2 shows that the `<user-card>` shadow DOM provides two slots, filled from the light DOM.

Listing 6-2. Slots with a Shadow DOM (chapter6/card/index.html)

```
<user-card>
  <span slot="username">Joerg</span>
  <span slot="birthday">May, 26</span>
</user-card>
<script>
customElements.define('user-card', class extends HTMLElement {
  connectedCallback() {
    this.attachShadow({mode: 'open'});
    this.shadowRoot.innerHTML = `
```

```
      <div>Name:
        <slot name="username"></slot>
      </div>
      <div>Birthday:
        <slot name="birthday"></slot>
      </div>
    `;
  }
});
</script>
```

Then the browser performs "composition:" it takes elements from the light DOM and renders them in corresponding slots of the Shadow DOM. At the end, you have exactly what you want: a component that can be filled with data.

Figure 6-2 shows the DOM structure after the script, not taking composition into account.

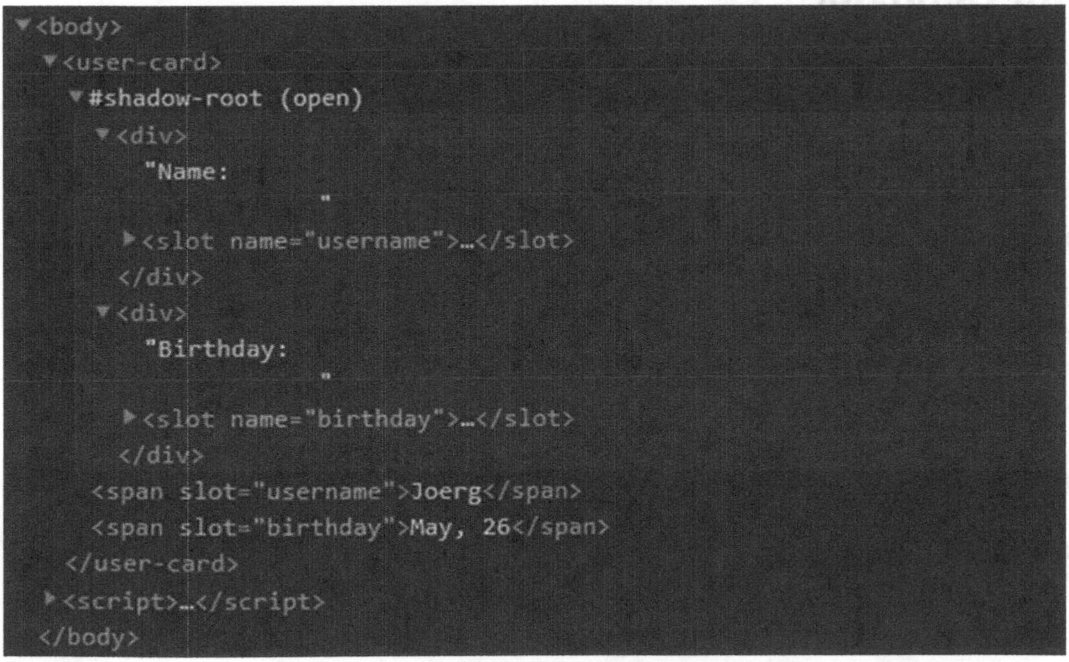

```
▼<body>
  ▼<user-card>
    ▼#shadow-root (open)
      ▼<div>
          "Name:
                              "
        ▶<slot name="username">…</slot>
        </div>
      ▼<div>
          "Birthday:
                              "
        ▶<slot name="birthday">…</slot>
        </div>
        <span slot="username">Joerg</span>
        <span slot="birthday">May, 26</span>
      </user-card>
  ▶<script>…</script>
  </body>
```

Figure 6-2. *Slots in a Web Component's Shadow DOM*

The shadow DOM is under `#shadow-root`. For rendering purposes, for each `<slot name="...">` in the Shadow DOM, the browser looks for *slot="..."* with the same name in the light DOM. These elements are rendered inside the slots. The flattened DOM exists only for rendering and event-handling purposes. It's kind of "virtual." That's how things are shown. But the nodes in the document are actually not moved around!

The last proposition can be easily checked if you run `querySelectorAll`. All the nodes are still at their places. The example shows that the light DOM `<span>` nodes are still at the same place, under `<user-card>`. Check it by executing this piece of code:

```
// Expected output: 2
console.log(document.querySelectorAll('user-card span').length );
```

So, the flattened DOM is derived from the Shadow DOM by inserting slots. The browser renders it and uses it for style inheritance and event propagation. But JavaScript's DOM API still sees the document "as is," before flattening.

Slot Behavior

In this section, I go a little deeper into the specific behaviors of slots.

Slot Positions

Only top-level children may have a *slot="..."* attribute. The *slot="..."* attribute is only valid for direct children of the shadow host (in this example, the `<user-card>` element). For nested elements, it's ignored.

In the example shown in Listing 6-3, the second `<span>` is ignored (as it's not a top-level child of `<user-card>`).

Listing 6-3. Nested Slots (chapter6/cardwrong/index.html)

```
<user-card>
  <span slot="username">Joerg Krause</span>
  <div>
    <!-- invalid slot, must be direct child of user-card →
    <span slot="birthday">May, 26</span>
  </div>
</user-card>
```

Multiple Slots

If there are multiple elements in a light DOM with the same slot name, they are appended into the slot, one after another. Listing 6-4 shows this and makes use of a list created by repeating slots.

Listing 6-4. Multiple Slots (chapter6/cardmany/index.html)

```
<user-card>
  <li slot="username">Joerg</li>
  <li slot="username">Clemens</li>
  <li slot="username">Elest</li>
  <span slot="birthday">May, 26</span>
</user-card>
<script>
  customElements.define(
    'user-card',
    class extends HTMLElement {
      connectedCallback() {
        this.attachShadow({ mode: 'open' });
        this.shadowRoot.innerHTML = `
        <div>Name:
          <ul>
            <slot name="username"></slot>
          </ul>
        </div>
        <div>Birthday:
          <slot name="birthday"></slot>
        </div>`;
      }
    }
  );
</script>
```

The <user-card> element is empty, so all slot content falls back to the default text provided in the slots' definitions. Figure 6-3 shows the outcome in the browser and debug view.

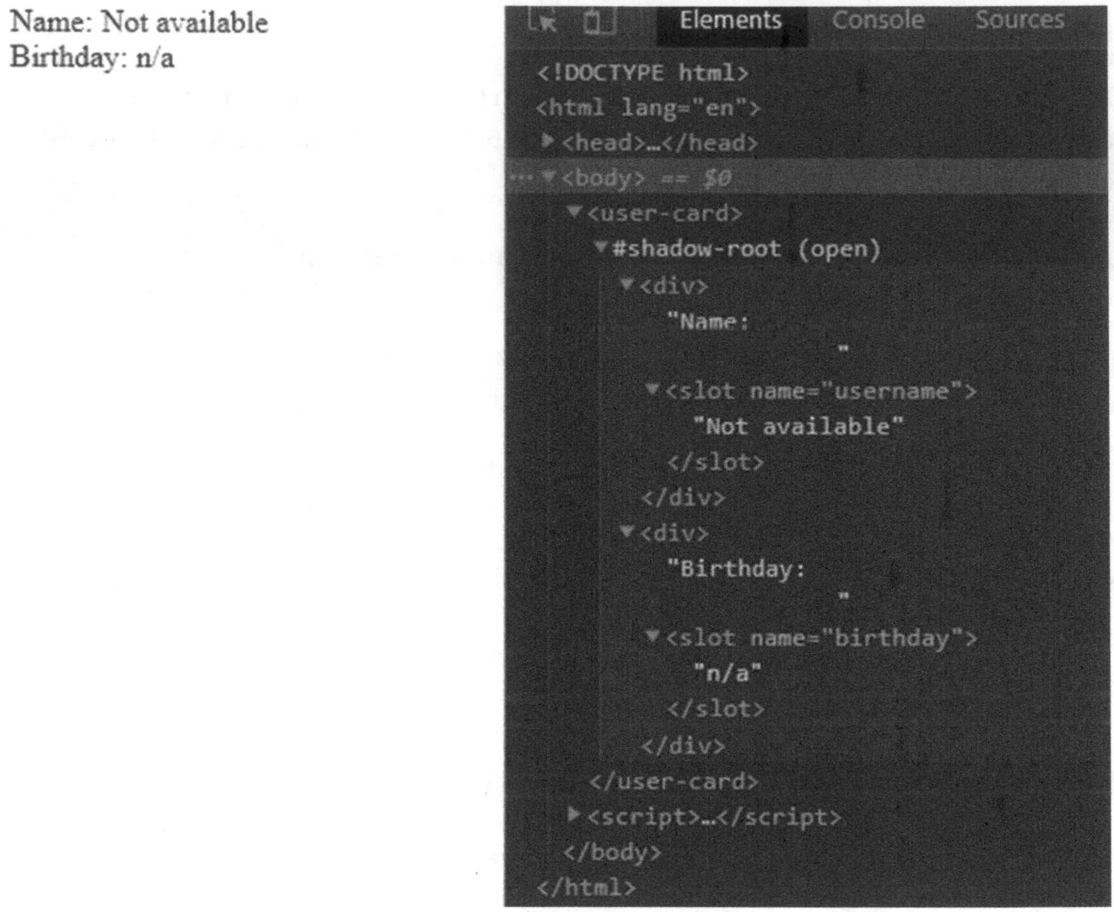

Name: Not available
Birthday: n/a

```
Elements    Console    Sources

<!DOCTYPE html>
<html lang="en">
  ▶ <head>…</head>
··· ▼ <body> == $0
    ▼ <user-card>
      ▼ #shadow-root (open)
        ▼ <div>
            "Name:
                      "
          ▼ <slot name="username">
              "Not available"
            </slot>
          </div>
        ▼ <div>
            "Birthday:
                      "
          ▼ <slot name="birthday">
              "n/a"
            </slot>
          </div>
        </user-card>
      ▶ <script>…</script>
      </body>
    </html>
```

Figure 6-3. *Fallback text appears if slots are missing*

Default Slots

The first `<slot>` in the Shadow DOM that doesn't have a name is a "default" slot. It gets all of the nodes from the light DOM that aren't slotted elsewhere.

For example, let's add the default slot to your `<user-card>` that shows all unslotted information about the user. See Listing 6-5.

Listing 6-5. Default Slot Content (chapter6/default/index.html)

```
<user-card></user-card>
<script>
  customElements.define(
    'user-card',
```

```
  class extends HTMLElement {
    connectedCallback() {
      this.attachShadow({ mode: 'open' });
      this.shadowRoot.innerHTML = `
    <div>Name:
      <slot name="username">Not available</slot>
    </div>
    <div>Birthday:
      <slot name="birthday">n/a</slot>
    </div>
    `;
    }
  }
);
</script>
```

All the unslotted light DOM content gets into the "Other information" fieldset (line 20).

Elements are appended to a slot one after another (see Figure 6-4), so both unslotted pieces of information are in the default slot together. The named slots are stripped out and placed where the placeholders are as before.

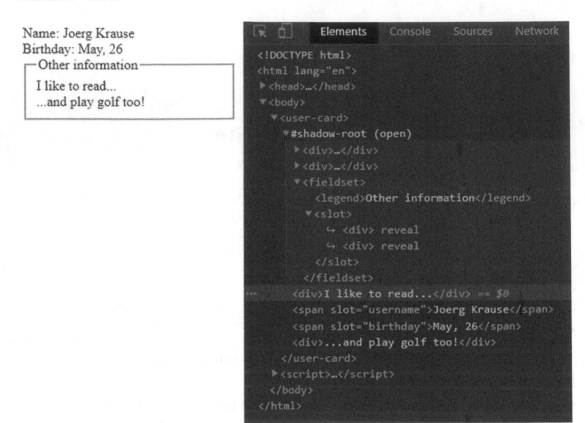

Figure 6-4. *Projected default content*

Slot Events

Now let's go back to the element `<custom-menu>`, mentioned at the beginning of this chapter. You can use slots to distribute menu items. Listing 6-6 shows the markup for `<custom-menu>`.

Listing 6-6. Custom Menu Items (chapter6/menu/index.html)

```
<custom-menu>
  <span slot="title">Technologies</span>
  <menu-item slot="item">HTML 5</menu-item>
  <menu-item slot="item">CSS 3</menu-item>
  <menu-item slot="item">ECMAScript</menu-item>
</custom-menu>
```

That's much better than the generic <li> in the slot elements. It requires, however, an additional component. The code has now two components; see Listing 6-7.

Listing 6-7. Slot Events (chapter6/menu/index.html)

```
customElements.define(
  'menu-item',
  class extends HTMLElement {
    connectedCallback() {
      this.attachShadow({ mode: 'open' });
      this.shadowRoot.innerHTML = `<li>${this.textContent}</li>`;
    }
  }
);
customElements.define(
  'custom-menu',
  class extends HTMLElement {
    connectedCallback() {
      this.attachShadow({ mode: 'open' });
      this.shadowRoot.innerHTML = `
    <div>
      <slot name="title"></div>
      <ul>
        <slot name="item"></slot>
      </ul>
    </div>
`;
    }
  }
);
```

The slots' content is not further abstracted. Instead, it's pulled directly as text using the textContent property.

Adding an Event Handler

As it is a menu, as a last step you need to add event handlers. That's not so much different from regular HTML, with just one exception. Attached event handlers are not copied in the clone process. Because slots need templates and templates need cloning, you must attach the events in the component and expose the event.

To expose custom events, you use the API call dispatchEvent like this:

```
customElements.define(
  'menu-item',
  class extends HTMLElement {
    connectedCallback() {
      this.attachShadow({ mode: 'open' });
      this.shadowRoot.innerHTML = `<li>${this.textContent}</li>`;
      this.shadowRoot.addEventListener('click', (e) => {
        if (e.target.tagName === 'LI') {
          console.log(e);
          this.dispatchEvent(new CustomEvent('menuclick', {
            details: e.currentTarget.textContent
          }));
        }
      });
    }
  }
);
```

The event name is your personal choice. It's as customizable as any name. If you want to transfer custom data, the class CustomEvent is better than just using Event. This type provides an additional property named detail. The receiving component must also access the content of the slot, not the actual definition. The complete example is written in TypeScript. Due to the types it gives a better understanding. See Listing 6-8.

Listing 6-8. Exposing an Event (chapter6/menuevent/event.ts)

```
class MenuItem extends HTMLElement {
  constructor() {
    super();
  }
```

```
  connectedCallback() {
    this.attachShadow({ mode: 'open' });
    if (this.shadowRoot) {
      this.shadowRoot.innerHTML = `<li>${this.textContent}</li>`;
      this.shadowRoot.addEventListener('click', (e: Event) => {
        if ((e.target as HTMLElement).tagName === 'LI') {
          console.log(e);
          const customEvent: CustomEventInit = {
            detail: (e.currentTarget as HTMLElement).textContent
          };
          this.dispatchEvent(new CustomEvent('menuclick', customEvent));
        }
      });
    }
  }
}

class CustomMenu extends HTMLElement {

  constructor() {
    super();
  }
  connectedCallback() {
    this.attachShadow({ mode: 'open' });
    if (this.shadowRoot) {
      this.shadowRoot.innerHTML = `
            <div>
              <slot name="title"></div>
              <ul>
                <slot name="item"></slot>
              </ul>
            </div>`;
      const slot = this
            .shadowRoot
            .querySelector<HTMLSlotElement>('slot[name="item"]');
```

```
      if (slot) {
        slot.assignedNodes()
          .forEach((e: Node) => {
            e.addEventListener('menuclick', (el: Event) =>
              alert((el as CustomEvent).detail));
          });
      }
    }
  }
}
customElements.define('menu-item', MenuItem);
customElements.define('custom-menu', CustomMenu);
```

In the event receiver, the slot is read by querySelector and the slot's selector (line 43). This returns an HTMLSlotElement instance. This is the same as HTMLElement with just one exception: the method assignedNodes. That's the way to access the projected content, the elements that fire the actual event. For all of the nodes, you attach an event handler that receives the custom event.

Custom events work exactly like the standard events, but they provide an additional field detail that can be of type any or a type enforced by a generic. To fire a custom event properly, the type CustomEventInit is the right way (line 14 to 17).

Updating Slots

Let's continue with the menu example. What if the outer code needs to add or remove menu items dynamically? The manipulation works as with any other element and goes directly into the DOM. Assume you have a single button on the page. The code in Listing 6-9 (lines 6 to 9) adds more items and re-renders the component immediately.

Listing 6-9. Exposing an Event (chapter6/menuevent/event.ts)

```
document.querySelector('button')?.addEventListener('click', () => {
  document.querySelector('custom-menu')?
    .insertAdjacentHTML('beforeend',
                        '<menu-item slot="item">This is new</menu-item>');
});
```

The components are the same as in the previous example.

Slot Change Events

If you want to monitor the changes, the API provides a special event, `slotchange` here. It fires one more than your actions because it also captures the initializing phase.

If you'd like to track the internal modifications of the light DOM from JavaScript, that's also possible using a more generic mechanism, the `MutationObserver`.

The Slot API

Finally, let's look into the slot-related JavaScript methods. As you've seen before, JavaScript looks at the "real" DOM, without flattening. But, if the shadow tree has `{mode: 'open'}`, you can figure out which elements are assigned to a slot and, vise-versa, the slot itself by the elements inside it:

- `node.assignedSlot`: Returns the `<slot>` element that the node is assigned to

- `slot.assignedNodes({flatten: true/false})`: DOM nodes assigned to the slot. The flatten option is `false` by default. If explicitly set to `true`, then it looks more deeply into the flattened DOM, returning nested slots in case of nested components and the fallback content if no node assigned.

- `slot.assignedElements({flatten: true/false})`: DOM elements assigned to the slot (same as above, but only element nodes)

These methods are useful when you don't just need to show the slotted content, but also track it in JavaScript. For example, if the `<custom-menu>` component wants to know what it shows, then it could track `slotchange` and get the items from `slot.assignedElements,` as in Listing 6-10.

Listing 6-10. Listening to an Event (chapter6/menuslotapi/event.ts)

```
this.shadowRoot
  .querySelector('ul')
  ?.addEventListener('slotchange', (s: Event) => {
    const slot = s.target as HTMLSlotElement;
```

```
  if (slot.name === 'item') {
    let items = slot.assignedElements()
      .map(e => e.textContent)
      .join(' ');
    const output = document.querySelector<HTMLDivElement>('#output');
    if (output) {
      output.innerText = items;
    }
  }
});
```

This is from the previously shown class called `CustomMenu`. First, the event source is the element where the slots' content is assigned. Here you capture the change (`<ul>`). The sender is the slot itself of type `HTMLSlotElement`. Using the method `assignedElements` you can get access to the actual element after the change happened. The rest of the code is just for demonstration. It retrieves the content and makes a visible output into a `<div>` element.

Summary

In this chapter, you captured the `<slot>` element and learned how to use it to parameterize templates. You explored some examples in JavaScript and TypeScript that showed the power of the underlying API, dealing with slot instances and handling slot-specific events.

CHAPTER 7

Components and Styles

Due to the fact that the DOM might be isolated, the styles are isolated too. The advantage is primarily the ability to use styles without knowing and disturbing any globally assigned styles. The disadvantage might be the reduced usability of global styles.

Style Behavior

A Shadow DOM may include both `<style>` and `<link rel="stylesheet" href="...">` tags. In the latter case, stylesheets are HTTP-cached, so they are not redownloaded for multiple components that use the same template.

As a general rule, local styles work only inside the shadow tree and document styles work outside of it. But there are a few exceptions.

Accessing the Host

The `:host` selector allows you to select the shadow host (the element containing the shadow tree).

For instance, let's say you're making a `<custom-dialog>` component that will be centered. For that you need to style the `<custom-dialog>` element itself.

That's exactly what `:host` does in Listing 7-1.

Listing 7-1. Applying the :host Selector (chapter7/host/index.html)

```
<template id="tmpl">
  <style>
    :host {
      position: fixed;
      left: 50%;
      top: 50%;
```

© Jörg Krause 2021
J. Krause, *Developing Web Components with TypeScript*, https://doi.org/10.1007/978-1-4842-6840-7_7

```
      transform: translate(-50%, -50%);
      display: inline-block;
      border: 1px solid red;
      padding: 10px;
    }
  </style>
  <slot></slot>
</template>

<script>
  customElements.define(
    'custom-dialog',
    class extends HTMLElement {
      connectedCallback() {
        this.attachShadow({ mode: 'open' }).append(tmpl.content.
        cloneNode(true));
      }
    }
  );
</script>

<custom-dialog> Hello! </custom-dialog>
```

While the component is shadowed, the styles still apply due to the selector in line 3.

Cascading

The shadow host (`<custom-dialog>` itself) resides in the light DOM, so it's affected by document CSS rules.

If there's a property styled both in `:host` locally and in the document, then the document style takes precedence.

For instance, assume in the document you had the style shown here:

```
<style>
  custom-dialog {
    padding: 0;
  }
</style>
```

In that case, the `<custom-dialog>` component would be without padding.

It's very convenient because you can set up "default" component styles in its `:host` rule and then easily override them in the document.

The exception is when a local property is labeled `!important`; for such properties, local styles take precedence. That's the normal CSS behavior. So if you intentionally want to change the order, add the `!important` label. This should be an exception, though.

Selecting a Host Element

Selecting a host element is the same as `:host`, but applied only if the shadow host matches the selector.

For example, say you'd like to center the `<custom-dialog>` only if it has a `centered` attribute, as shown in Listing 7-2.

Listing 7-2. Applying the :host Selector (chapter7/select/index.html)

```
<template id="tmpl">
  <style>
    :host([centered]) {
      position: fixed;
      left: 50%;
      top: 50%;
      transform: translate(-50%, -50%);
      border-color: blue;
    }

    :host {
      display: inline-block;
      border: 1px solid red;
      padding: 10px;
    }
  </style>
  <slot></slot>
</template>
```

```
<script>
  customElements.define(
    'custom-dialog',
    class extends HTMLElement {
      connectedCallback() {
        this.attachShadow({ mode: 'open' }).append(tmpl.content.
        cloneNode(true));
      }
    }
  );
</script>

<custom-dialog centered> Centered! </custom-dialog>

<custom-dialog> Not centered. </custom-dialog>
```

Now the additional centering styles are only applied to the first dialog, `<custom-dialog centered>`.

It's a smart technique that unleashes the power of CSS on the level of custom attributes. In bigger and hence more complex applications it's an advantage to avoid the usage of multiple `data-` attributes and nested classes and to replace them with simple top-level attributes. However, you should try to find a balance between those techniques. Creating a style system that is very closely bound to Web Components might be attractive at first glance. But the further away you go from established CSS, the bigger the risk is that using existing sets of style rules is almost impossible.

Accessing the Host Context Aware

There is another selector named `:host-context` that brings even more control. Using `:host-context(selector)` is done the same way as `:host`, but it's applied only if the shadow host or any of its ancestors in the outer document matches the selector.

For example, `:host-context(.dark-theme)` matches only if there's a `dark-theme` class on `<custom-dialog>` or anywhere above it (see Listing 7-3).

Listing 7-3. Applying the :host-context Selector (chapter7/context/index.html)

```
<body class="dark-theme">
  <!--
    :host-context(.dark-theme) applies to custom-dialogs inside .dark-theme
  -->
  <custom-dialog>...</custom-dialog>
</body>
```

To summarize, you can use the :host family of selectors to style the main element of the component, depending on the context. These styles (unless !important) can be overridden by the document.

Styling Slotted Content

Now let's consider the situation with slots. Slots are explained in great detail in Chapter 6. Slotted elements come from the light DOM, so they use document styles. Local styles do not affect slotted content.

In Listing 7-4, the slotted <span> is bold, as per the document style, but it does not take a background from the local style.

Listing 7-4. Using Slots (chapter7/slots/index.html)

```
<style>
  span {
    font-weight: bold;
  }
</style>

<user-card>
  <div slot="username"><span>Joerg Krause</span></div>
</user-card>

<script>
  customElements.define(
    'user-card',
```

```
  class extends HTMLElement {
    connectedCallback() {
      this.attachShadow({ mode: 'open' });
      this.shadowRoot.innerHTML = `
    <style>
    span { background: red; }
    </style>
    Name: <slot name="username"></slot>
  `;
    }
  }
);
</script>
```

The result is bold, but not red. If you'd like to style slotted elements in your component, there are two choices.

First, you can style the <slot> itself and rely on CSS inheritance as shown in Listing 7-5.

Listing 7-5. Using Slots (chapter7/slotin/index.html)

```
<user-card>
  <div slot="username"><span>Joerg Krause</span></div>
</user-card>

<script>
  customElements.define(
    'user-card',
    class extends HTMLElement {
      connectedCallback() {
        this.attachShadow({ mode: 'open' });
        this.shadowRoot.innerHTML = `
      <style>
      slot[name="username"] { font-weight: bold; }
      </style>
      Name: <slot name="username"></slot>
    `;
```

```
        }
      }
  );
</script>
```

Here `<p>Joerg Krause</p>` becomes bold because CSS inheritance is in effect between the `<slot>` and its contents. But in CSS itself not all properties are inherited.

Another option is to use the `::slotted(selector)` pseudo selector. It matches elements based on two conditions:

1. It must be a slotted element that comes from the light DOM. The slot's name doesn't matter. It behaves like any slotted element, but only the element itself is seen by the selector, not its children.

2. The element matches the selector.

In this example, `::slotted(div)` selects exactly `<div slot="username">`, but not its children, as shown in Listing 7-6.

Listing 7-6. Using Slots (chapter7/slotted/index.html)

```html
<user-card>
  <div slot="username">
    <div>Joerg Krause</div>
  </div>
</user-card>

<script>
  customElements.define(
    'user-card',
    class extends HTMLElement {
      connectedCallback() {
        this.attachShadow({ mode: 'open' });
        this.shadowRoot.innerHTML = `
      <style>
      ::slotted(div) { border: 1px solid red; }
      </style>
      Name: <slot name="username"></slot>
      `;
```

```
      }
    }
  );
</script>
```

Please note that the `::slotted` pseudo selector can't descend any further into the slot. The following selectors are invalid:

```
::slotted(div span) {
  /* our slotted <div> does not match this */
}
```

```
::slotted(div) p {
  /* can't go inside light DOM */
}
```

Also, `::slotted` can only be used in CSS. You can't use it in `querySelector` to select. That's not specific to Web Components: pseudo selectors can't be used to select elements using the integrated selector API.

The selector behavior is slightly different from libraries such as Sizzle (part of jQuery). Those libraries add some non-standard behavior and provide selector options the browser API doesn't have. But I think that staying with the standard is the better option so avoid using such libraries just for convenience. If you need additional selections, add custom attributes.

CSS Hooks

To style internal elements of a component from the main document, you can use additional hooks. Selectors like `:host` apply rules to `<custom-dialog>` element or `<user-card>`, but how to style shadow DOM elements inside them?

There's no selector that can directly affect shadow DOM styles from the document. But just as you expose methods to interact with your component, you can expose CSS variables (custom CSS properties) to style it. Custom CSS properties exist on all parts, both in light and Shadow DOMs.

For example, in the Shadow DOM you can use the `--user-card-field-color` CSS variable to style fields and the outer document can set its value:

```
<style>
  .field {
    color: var(--user-card-field-color, black);
    /* if --user-card-field-color is not defined, use black color */
  }
</style>
<div class="field">Name: <slot name="username"></slot></div>
<div class="field">Birthday: <slot name="birthday"></slot></div>
```

Then, you can declare this property in the outer document for `<user-card>`:

```
user-card {
  --user-card-field-color: green;
}
```

Custom CSS properties "pierce" through the Shadow DOM. They are visible everywhere, so the inner `.field` class will make use of them. Listing 7-7 shows the full example.

Listing 7-7. CSS Hooks (chapter7/hooks/index.html)

```
<style>
  user-card {
    --user-card-field-color: green;
  }
</style>

<template id="tmpl">
  <style>
    .field {
      color: var(--user-card-field-color, black);
    }
  </style>
  <div class="field">Name: <slot name="username"></slot></div>
  <div class="field">Birthday: <slot name="birthday"></slot></div>
</template>
```

105

```
<script>
  customElements.define(
    'user-card',
    class extends HTMLElement {
      connectedCallback() {
        this.attachShadow({ mode: 'open' });
        this.shadowRoot.append(document.getElementById('tmpl').content.
        cloneNode(true));
      }
    }
  );
</script>
<user-card>
  <span slot="username">Joerg Krause</span>
  <span slot="birthday">May, 26</span>
</user-card>
```

Ignoring Styles

I discussed the possibility of copying global styles into the component at the beginning of this chapter. That's a primitive technique and contradicts the isolation principle. However, sometimes it might be good to do this selectively. Following the pattern of the pseudo selectors shown before, you could add a "custom" pseudo selector. Browsers will simply ignore it. You can add the pseudo style :ignore to global styles, for example:

```
div.special:ignore {
  font-weight: bold;
}
```

This style will not be copied, then. It works in the browser as before because the not-normative pseudo is ignored. You may wonder why it works, since I said that pseudo selectors can't be used as selection criteria. That's true, but only for those supported by the standard. When it comes to pseudo-pseudo-selectors, they seem to work as part of the rule name. But keep an eye on this because future implementations may change the browsers' behaviors.

Parts

The Shadow DOM is a specification that provides DOM and style encapsulation. This is great for reusable Web Components because it reduces the possibility of these components' styles getting accidentally stomped on, but it adds a barrier for styling and theming these components deliberately. In developer terms, it's like having namespaces for isolation but no proper import statement to use them selectively.

Please note that this standardization process isn't quite final, which means that the syntax and capabilities will likely change and there isn't a polyfill you can use right now. I suggest proper testing (or prototyping) before putting too much effort into a project.

When styling a component, there are usually two different problems you want to solve:

- **Styling**: You want to use a third-party `<fancy-button>` element on your site and you want it to be blue.

- **Theming**: You want to use many third-party elements on a site. Some of them have a `<fancy-button>` and all of the `<fancy-button>` components must be blue.

In older literature, you may find `:shadow` and `/deep/`. They were shadow-piercing selectors that allowed you to target any node in a component's Shadow DOM. Apart from being bad for performance, they also required the user of an element to be intimately familiar with the component's implementation. Nowadays both selectors are deprecated.

Let's look into an example with properties:

```
fancy-button#one {
  --fancy-button-background: blue;
}
fancy-button {
  --fancy-button-background: blue;
}
```

The problem with using just custom properties for styling or theming is that it places the onus on the element author to basically declare every possible styleable property as a custom property.

The Part Attribute and Pseudo Selector

Another way to style elements from outside the Shadow DOM is `::part`, a set of pseudo-elements that use a related part attribute. You can specify a "styleable" part on any element in your shadow tree by using the part attribute like this:

```
<my-part>
  #shadow-root
  <div part="some-box"><span>...</span></div>
  <input part="some-input" />
  <div>...</div>
  <!-- not styleable -->
</my-part>
```

The part marked as `#shadow-root` is the content of the my-part Web Component. You can style these parts with the selector like this:

```
my-part::part(some-box) {
  ...;
}
```

This is different from a typical attribute selector, which can select an element by an attribute but won't cross Shadow DOM boundaries, hence the need for a special pseudo selector here. You can use other pseudo elements or selectors (that were not explicitly exposed as shadow parts), so both of these options work:

```
my-part::part(some-box):hover {
  ...;
}
my-part::part(some-input)::placeholder {
  ...;
}
```

You can't select inside of those parts, so the following example doesn't work:

```
my-part::part(some-box) span {
  ...;
}
nor my-part::part(some-box)::part(some-other-thing) {
  ...;
}
```

You can't style this part more than one level up if you don't forward it. So without any extra work, if you have an element that contains a my-part like

```
<my-bar>
  #shadow-root
  <my-part></my-part>
</my-bar>
```

you cannot select and style the my-part component's part like

```
my-bar::part(some-box) {
  ...;
}
```

See Listing 7-8.

Listing 7-8. Parts in Action (chapter7/parts/index.html)

```
<style>
    app-tabs::part(tab) {
      color: #0c0dcc;
      border-bottom: transparent solid 2px;
    }
    app-tabs::part(tab):hover {
      background-color: silver;
      border-color: #0a84ff;
    }
```

```css
    app-tabs::part(active) {
      color: #0060df;
      border-color: #0a84ff !important;
    }
</style>
<template id="tabtemplate">
    <style type="text/css">
      *,
      ::before,
      ::after {
        box-sizing: border-box;
        padding: 1rem;
      }
      :host {
        display: flex;
      }
    </style>
    <div part="tab active">Tab 1</div>
    <div part="tab">Tab 2</div>
    <div part="tab">Tab 3</div>
  </template>
<app-tabs></app-tabs>
<script>
    let template = document.querySelector("#tabtemplate");
    customElements.define("app-tabs", class extends HTMLElement {
      constructor() {
        super();
        this.attachShadow({ mode: "open" });
        this.shadowRoot.appendChild(template.content);
        this.shadowRoot.querySelectorAll('[part]').forEach(part => {
          part.addEventListener('click', e => {
            this.shadowRoot.querySelectorAll('[part]')
                .forEach(e => e.part.remove('active'));
            e.target.part.add('active');
          });
```

```
    });
  }
});
</script>
```

This is a simple tab user interface that uses the `part` attribute to control the styles. The styles are partially inside (general ones) and mostly outside to let the one using the component control the final appearance.

In the browser's debug view you can easily see the final form the browser has interpreted.

The interesting behavior here is the way the `part` attribute works. It's very much like the `class` attribute: if the value contains names separated by spaces, the `::part` pseudo selector can address each of these names individually. In the example, it's `tab` and `active`, respectively.

Also, you can use other pseudo selectors to further refine the styles for such parts, as shown with `hover` in the example:

```
app-tabs::part(tab):hover
The same would work for other selectors, such as "::placeholder" or
"::selection".
```

Forwarding Parts

You can explicitly forward a child's part to be styleable outside of the parent's shadow tree with the `exportparts` attribute. That means an inner part that would not be accessible from the outside otherwise is opened so an external style can reach it.

As an extension to the previous example, you can allow the part to be styleable by the parent by exposing the inner part as "`some-box`" like this:

```
<my-bar>
  #shadow-root
  <my-part exportparts="some-box"></my-part>
</my-bar>
```

The `exportparts` forwarding syntax has several options. You can simply export, export partially, or export and rename the exported part. The next example shows a usage scenario. The export part looks like this:

```
<app-tabs exportparts="tab: currenttab, active"></app-tabs>
```

Here the part tab of the inner element gets a new name, currenttab. The part active of the inner element is forwarded directly, keeping its name. This is useful for avoiding name conflicts in CSS, which otherwise would be hard to deal with because of the lack of namespaces. See Listing 7-9.

Listing 7-9. Parts in Action (chapter7/exportparts/index.html)

```
<style>
  app-tab-menu::part(currenttab) {
    color: #0c0dcc;
    border-bottom: transparent solid 2px;
  }
  app-tab-menu::part(currenttab):hover {
    background-color: silver;
    border-color: #0a84ff;
  }
  app-tab-menu::part(active) {
    color: #0060df;
    border-color: #0a84ff !important;
  }
</style>
<template id="tabtemplate">
  <style type="text/css">
    *,
    ::before,
    ::after {
      box-sizing: border-box;
      padding: 1rem;
    }

    :host {
      display: flex;
    }
  </style>
  <div part="tab active">Tab 1</div>
  <div part="tab">Tab 2</div>
```

```
  <div part="tab">Tab 3</div>
</template>

<template id="tabmenu">
  <app-tabs exportparts="tab: currenttab, active"></app-tabs>
</template>

<app-tab-menu></app-tab-menu>

<script>
  customElements.define("app-tabs", class extends HTMLElement {
    constructor() {
      super();
      this.attachShadow({ mode: "open" });
      this.shadowRoot.appendChild(document.querySelector("#tabtemplate").
      content);
      this.shadowRoot.querySelectorAll('[part]').forEach(part => {
        part.addEventListener('click', e =>  {
          this.shadowRoot.querySelectorAll('[part]')
              .forEach(e => e.part.remove('active'));
          e.target.part.add('active');
        });
      });
    }
  });
  customElements.define("app-tab-menu", class extends HTMLElement {
    constructor() {
      super();
      this.attachShadow({ mode: "open" });
      this.shadowRoot.appendChild(document.querySelector("#tabmenu").
      content);
    }
  });
</script>
```

The example in Listing 7-9 is similar to the previous one in Listing 7-8. It's now split in two nested components, and the inner parts are piped through the outer component using the `exportparts` attribute. This way the appearance of the part names can be managed by the outer component, adapting to existing styles, resolving name conflicts, or just for the sake of readability.

The Part API

The `click` event and the code around this part controls the part values directly. Here you can see the associated API for handling parts. The property `part` contains an object of type `DOMTokenList` that allows you to handle the part values individually. It's not specific to the parts here but is nonetheless useful for working with multiple values. The behavior is identical to the property `classList`.

You can find more about this type at `https://developer.mozilla.org/en/docs/Web/API/DOMTokenList.`

Please note that the compatibility list on that page shows the general availability of `DOMTokenList` in a browser, not the ability to use it with the part attributes.

The Future of Parts

Some sources available online propose further features. One is the handling of themes by using another pseudo selector, `::theme`. Also, there is a suggestion that the export of parts could be handled by an asterisk (`exportparts="*"`). Neither of these ideas made it into the major browsers and it's unclear when this is going to happen.

If a majority of front-end developers are moving from JavaScript frameworks to Web Components, then it would be useful to get more features. The applications will become more complex and feature-rich, and Web Components will play a central role in the development cycle. But nowadays the fate of Web Components is to provide an isolated piece of a user interface, a fragment of a bigger app, or just an extension to a framework-based solution. You'll hardly need more than a few parts. And that's already feasible with what the browser vendors provide today[1].

---

[1]Written in the beginning of 2021.

Summary

In this chapter, I covered how to add cascading style sheets to Web Components. You saw how to pierce the isolation boundary and deal with several pseudo selectors to make components styleable and themeable. I also added some advice for using the underlying API. Some parts of the standards are under active development currently and those parts were discussed only briefly.

CHAPTER 8

Making Single-Page Apps

A single-page application (SPA) is a web application or website that interacts with the web browser by dynamically refreshing part of the current web page with new data from the web server, instead of the default method of the browser loading entire new pages. The goal is faster transitions that make the website feel more like a native app.

In an SPA, all necessary HTML, JavaScript, and CSS code is either retrieved by the browser with a single page load, or the appropriate resources are dynamically loaded and added to the page as necessary, usually in response to user actions. The page does not reload at any point in the process, nor does it transfer control to another page, although the location hash or the HTML5 History API can be used to provide the perception and navigability of separate logical pages in the application. The history API makes the browser's navigation buttons work properly.

The Architecture of SPAs

SPAs consist of several parts and layers. I will briefly explain all parts shortly.

The Router

Usually, when you create SPAs you use a router. While it sounds complicated, in reality it isn't. Of course, you can add tons of features, but the basic behavior is always the same. The basic function consists of two parts:

- Monitoring the navigation URL
- Defining a target location for the replaceable part

© Jörg Krause 2021
J. Krause, *Developing Web Components with TypeScript*, https://doi.org/10.1007/978-1-4842-6840-7_8

An SPA can be made without a router. The router is just an architectural pattern that's suitable for small- and medium-size applications. If you have a very big implementation, a state engine and more specialized solutions would suit better. The difficulty starts if you need to have routing that handles authentication and here a simple router will start mixing up business logic, state, and navigation logic.

Monitoring the URL

In an SPA you don't care about the full URL. To prevent the browser from navigating away, the router instruction is delivered using a hash value ('#value'). If that hash changes, the appropriate event fires.

Hash   The hash property of the URL is a string containing a # followed by the fragment identifier of the URL. It's used to navigate "in-page" and prevent the browser from requesting content from the server. The usage in router logic is a little misuse of an existing feature. It is, however, safe to use and available in all environments.

To monitor the URL's hash you can use an event like the one shown in Listing 8-1.

Listing 8-1. Monitoring Hash Change Events

```
function locationHashChanged(e) {
  if (location.hash === '#pageX') {
    // invoke router logic
  }
}

window.addEventListener('hashchange') = (e) => locationHashChanged(e);
```

As you can see in Listing 8-1, the hash value determines the action. A router usually has a router configuration that is simply a dictionary with the hash values and the components' types.

Some router libraries distinguish between hash routing (as shown here) and location routing (full URL changes). Location routing is possible with HTML 5 base URL features. The advantage is that location routing is a bit more search engine-friendly. Hash routing is, on the other hand, easier to implement and more robust.

Because you are creating components on the fly, you can't provide dynamic data for attributes. It makes sense to have some sort of common order for your project to achieve a good router.

```
|- main component
|
|--- home page component
  |
  |- some page component
  |   |
  |   \- business component
  |
  \- some page component
```

The router will load just containers. Their whole purpose is to serve as a starting point for your business components. Such containers have no code, no attributes, and return the basic structure of an application fragment.

Configuring the Router

The easiest way to configure a router is a simple dictionary. This could be dynamic, loaded from JSON, based on certain circumstances, or simply an object defined in the main component. The code in Listing 8-2 shows how to register routes.

Listing 8-2. Router Configuration

```
const routes = {
  '': { component: DemoComponent },
  '#about': { component: AboutComponent },
  '#demo': { component: DemoComponent },
```

```
  '#contact': { component: ContactComponent },
  '**': { component: DemoComponent },
};
```

Defining the Target

The target is usually called an outlet. The placement of a component is a simple DOM operation. The first step is removing the probably existing component. In a second step the new component is added. The browser's engine takes care of the render process.

To define an outlet where the components appear, you can either use existing elements or a component. The example in this chapter uses another component like this:

`<app-router-outlet></app-router-outlet>`

The outlet must know when the user clicks somewhere, changing the URL and depending on that URL pulling the right component and adding it to the DOM.

As shown in the previous section, it's easy to monitor the navigation URL.

Router Implementation

Now that you know the technical base, it's time to implement. The full example in Listing 8-3 is written in TypeScript and for the sake of simplicity in just one file. It consists of these parts:

- A main component with navigation links

- The router outlet with routing logic

- Three demo components that deliver content

To work with this example, don't forget to transpile first using the `tsc` command.

Listing 8-3. Full Router App (chapter8/router/all.components.ts)

```typescript
export type Type<T> = new (...args: any[]) => T;

class Page1Component extends HTMLElement {
  connectedCallback() {
    this.innerHTML = 'Page One';
  }
}
```

```
class Page2Component extends HTMLElement {
  connectedCallback() {
    this.innerHTML = 'Page Two';
  }
}

class Page3Component extends HTMLElement {
  connectedCallback() {
    this.innerHTML = 'Page Three';
  }
}

class MainComponent extends HTMLElement {

  constructor() {
    super();
  }

  render() {
    this.innerHTML = `
    <h1>Single Page Demo</h1>
    <nav>
      <a href="#page1">Page 1</a> |
      <a href="#page2">Page 2</a> |
      <a href="#page3">Page 3</a> |
    </nav>
    <div class="container">
      <app-router-outlet></app-router-outlet>
    </div>
    `;
  }

  connectedCallback() {
    this.render();
  }
}
```

```typescript
class RouterOutletComponent extends HTMLElement {

  private routes: { [path: string]: Type<HTMLElement> }

  constructor() {
    super();
    this.routes = {
      '': Page1Component,
      '#page1': Page1Component,
      '#page2': Page2Component,
      '#page3': Page3Component
    };
  }

  connectedCallback() {
    window.addEventListener('hashchange',
      (e: HashChangeEvent) => this.locationHashChanged(e));
  }

  disconnectedCallback() {
    window.removeEventListener('hashchange',
      (e: HashChangeEvent) => this.locationHashChanged(e));
  }

  locationHashChanged(e: HashChangeEvent) {
    const paths = Object.keys(this.routes);
    if (paths.some(r => r === window.location.hash)) {
      this.innerHTML = '';
      const type = this.routes[window.location.hash];
      const component = new type;
      this.insertAdjacentElement('afterbegin', component);
    }
  }

}

customElements.define('app-main', MainComponent);
customElements.define('app-router-outlet', RouterOutletComponent);
```

```
customElements.define('app-page1', Page1Component);
customElements.define('app-page2', Page2Component);
customElements.define('app-page3', Page3Component);
```

The code in Listing 8-3 works when called from a simple HTML page, as shown in Listing 8-4. Let's investigate the crucial parts here. Since you're using TypeScript, the typing is critical. The type definition helps the transpiler to understand that the given type can be instantiated (line 1). In the router dictionary (line 32) you place the pure type objects and later create an instance by calling the new operator. The dictionary definition is on line 48:

```
private routes: { [path: string]: Type<HTMLElement> }
```

The event for monitoring hash changes is added in connectedCallback. It's being removed in case you disconnect later. That's not necessary in such a simple app, but in reality it will grow and then even the parent element could be dynamic. So you need to take care of the event handlers to avoid memory leaks. Quite often you'll face situations where some sort of child routing is necessary and multiple outlets are being targeted.

The actual component exchange consists of three steps. First, in line 72 you look for a valid route. Consider adding a fallback here to capture wrongly constructed links. Second, the current content of the router is removed. Third, the actual type is retrieved, instantiated (line 75), and inserted into the DOM (line 73). The browser renders it and it appears immediately.

Listing 8-4. Router App Startup File (chapter8/router/all.components.ts)

```html
<!DOCTYPE html>
<html lang="en">
  <head>
    <meta charset="UTF-8" />
    <meta name="viewport" content="width=device-width, initial-scale=1.0" />
    <title>Mini Router</title>
    <style>
      * {
        font-family: sans-serif;
      }
```

```
    .container {
      padding: 15px;
    }
    nav {
      padding: 10px;
      border: solid gray 1px;
    }
  </style>
</head>
<body>
  <app-main></app-main>
  <script src="all.component.js"></script>
</body>
</html>
```

In the beginning, the outlet is empty and no page is shown. If you want to fall back to Page1Component, the following code will do the trick:

```
<div class="container">
  <app-router-outlet>
    <app-page1></app-page1>
  </app-router-outlet>
</div>
```

Figure 8-1 shows the result of the demo application.

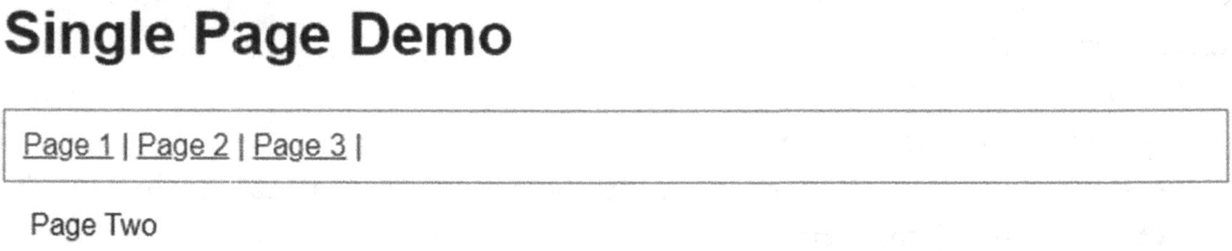

Single Page Demo

Page 1 | Page 2 | Page 3 |

Page Two

Figure 8-1. *The router demo in action*

The History API

The HTML5 history API gives you access to the browser navigation history via JavaScript. The HTML5 history API is really useful in single-page web apps. A single-page app can use the API to make a certain state in the app available for bookmarking and for navigation with respective buttons.

The History Stack

The browsing history consists of a stack of URLs. Every time the user navigates within the *same website*, the URL of the new page is placed at the top of the stack. When the user clicks the "back" button, the pointer in the stack is moved to the previous element on the stack. If the user clicks the "forward" button again, the pointer is moved forward to the top-most element on the stack. If the user clicks "back" and then clicks on a new link, the top-most element on the stack will be overwritten with the new URL.

The history Object

You access the browsing history via the history object, which is available as a global object.

The history object contains the following functions:

- back()
- forward()
- go(index)
- pushState(stateObject, title, url)
- replaceState(stateObject, title, url)

The back function moves the browsing history back to the previous URL. Calling back has the same effect as if the user clicked the browser's "back" button.

The forward function moves the browsing history forward to the next page in the history. Calling forward has the same effect as clicking the browser's "forward" button. This is only possible if the back function has been called before or if the "back" button has been clicked. If the history already points to the latest URL in the browsing history, there is nothing to move forward to.

The go(index) function can move the history either backward or forward depending on the index you pass as parameter to the function. If you call it with a negative index (e.g. go(-1)), then the browser moves backward in history. If you pass a positive index to the function, then the browser moves forward in the browsing history (e.g. go(1)). The index indicates how many steps in the history to move either forward or backward.

The pushState(stateObject, title, url) function pushes a new URL onto the history stack. The function takes three parameters. The url is the URL to push onto the history stack. The title parameter is mostly ignored by the browsers. The stateObject is an object that is passed along with the event fired when a new URL is pushed onto the history stack. This stateObject can contain any data you want. It is just a JavaScript object. This function is probably the most important to use with the router because it allows you to add states even if the internal behavior does not recognize the action made in code accordingly.

The replaceState(stateObject, title, url) function works like the pushState function except it replaces the current element in the history stack with a new URL. The current element is not necessarily the top element. It is the element currently being pointed to, which can be any element in the stack, if the back, forward, and go functions have been called on the history object.

History Change Events

The HTML5 history API enables a web page to listen for changes in the browser history. The security restrictions apply here too, so a web page will not be notified of history changes that lead to URLs outside of the domain of the web page.

To listen for changes in the browser history, you set an onpopstate listener on the window object. Here is a browser history event listener example:

```
window.onpopstate = function (event) {
  console.log('history changed to: ' + document.location.href);
};
```

The onpopstate event handler function will get called every time the browser history changes within the same page (the browser history that page pushed onto the history stack). The reaction to a history change event could be to extract parameters from the URL and load the corresponding content into the page (e.g. via AJAX).

Only changes caused by either the "back" or "forward" buttons or the corresponding history navigation functions back, forward, and go will cause the onpopstate event listener to get called. Calling the pushState and replaceState functions will not cause a history change event to be fired.

Final Thoughts on the History API

As you can see, creating a router for SPA is very easy and there is no need to work with a full blown framework for just this single task. All you need is a basic understanding of the HTML 5 API and, of course, Web Components. One thing could be a little bit more challenging, though. Adding and removing components means that the instances are being unloaded and destroyed. You can see this if you put an output in the disconnectCallback methods. This means the components are stateless. While the whole application stays in memory all the time, the finally working components are ephemeral.

What you need here to solve this is a global state. That's the purpose of the Flux architecture: writing stateful applications. I capture this in the next section and it will be less complicated than you think.

Stateful Apps

Some time ago someone wrote that the only reason to use a full front-end framework is to keep the application's state. Keeping a global and central state is a very crucial part of an SPA. As you saw in the previous section, the components are ephemeral. They load and unload as the user clicks through the application's UI. Keeping a state is necessary to avoid endless round-trips to the server. Of course, there are some APIs you can use, such as *localStorage*. But this would result in a deep coupling between components. Any component that wants to consume a certain state must exactly know how another component has written this value. **Tight coupling is the mother of all software hell.** Any change will lead to an endless chain of changes, and in a usually surprisingly short period of time the software will become a mess nobody can handle anymore.

A global state solves this by putting all values in a central space and letting all components access it in a well-defined way. Because there are many ways to implement such a thing and as many to use it, it would be good to have a distinct architectural pattern for this task. The architecture we use nowadays to achieve the goal of a stateful application is called *Flux*.

127

Flux was first described by Facebook in 2013 while presenting the first version of React. React is a component library and the developers faced the very same problem: How to keep the state?

Flux

The Flux pattern is not just the state. It also provides a well-defined way to handle the business logic. The components you have seen so far are just pieces of the user interface (UI), also called views. Because it's code, you can place actual business logic in it. But this feels bad because it violates another principle called "the separation of concerns." Following this principle, you should not mix view code (UI) with logic code. Putting the logic outside the component is easy by using services, but this would again create a tight coupling between the components and their services. Hence, one problem solved and another one increased.

The Flux architecture solves this by introducing a very smart way of handling the state changes using logic outside of components. First, let's look at a simple chart, shown in Figure 8-2.

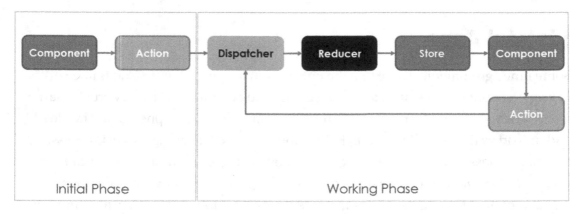

Figure 8-2. *Simple view of the Flux architecture*

The main principle is the data flow. It's always unidirectional. The data come in a specific way into the store and from there to the component. The store is not directly accessible. Such a protected store is very reliable, hence it is often called **the single source of truth**. So, whatever is going on in your app, the store knows, and all other parts can ask the store, and nobody else can change it.

The Flux Parts

To make this work, you need few parts with very clear tasks:

- **Actions** that define tasks (such as SEARCH, LOAD, SET, REMOVE, you name it)

- **Reducers** that are pure function calls that do what your business logic requires (change data, call services)

- A **Store** that holds all the data. The reducer can request a change of state, but nobody else can.

In the component you have two possible options:

- Call a **Dispatcher** by sending actions along with an (optional) payload.

- Listen for changes from a **Subscriber** in the store to know when a reducer has finished its task.

This sounds complicated and the amount of boilerplate code is significant. But the outcome is outstanding. Using a Flux model improves the code quality dramatically, the strictness and clearness of the code is astonishing, and the ability to handle huge applications is a big step forward.

It takes some time to understand the pattern and deal with it fluently. It's definitely worth the effort.

Tell Tales

The first Flux implementation was quite complicated and soon developers ditched the proposal, not seeing it as a real advantage. On top of this, several store libraries appeared that had a simpler API, reduced functions, or a more clever approach to handling the data. One of the well-known libraries is called *Redux*. But there are several others. Most are independent of a certain framework; some are bound to a specific one (Redux is for React, NgRX is the same for Angular, MobX is an independent one, for example).

Proposition   Anything that can be derived from the application state should be
derived. Automatically.

Implementing Flux

In this chapter, I'm going to show how to implement such a pattern from scratch. No
library, no framework. It's a good starter for learning and often more than enough for
real-life projects. It's a few more lines of code, but worth the effort to browse through the
lines.

This example is split into multiple files and hence needs a loader technique.
Fortunately, you can use the ES2016 module concept that nowadays all browsers support
using `<script type="module">`. But nothing good is without a pitfall. Loading from file
is not possible due to CORS (cross-origin resource sharing) issues. That means you must
load the example through HTTP. For that reason, the example code includes an HTTP
server. Use **$ npm start** to start the script and navigate to the examples.

The code also doesn't use any packer (such as WebPack), hence nothing is resolving
the module files' extensions. This is not exactly how it works in real-life TypeScript
projects with multiple files, but it reduces the amount of boilerplate code drastically.
Hence the import statements look like this:

```
import { Observer, callBackType } from './observer.js';
```

The difference is the trailing `.js` that the ES2016 module loader requires and what an
ordinary packer like WebPack would not need. Again, that's to simplify the demo. **If you
take over the code to a real project, you must remove the file extensions!**

Overview

The example consists of three parts:

1. A Web Component to start the application

2. The store implementation

3. An observer for a publish/subscribe pattern

The publish/subscribe pattern is the underlying technique to communicate with the store. It allows the component to subscribe to store changes and refresh the UI when that happens. The store itself monitors the changes initiated by reducers and invokes the publish method. The observer is a simple class, not an external library. The whole code has no dependencies.

Why not use Promise?   The Promise class supports a one-time operation only. If it's done, it's gone. This means the subscriber must subscribe again after receiving a call. This is at least not very convenient. That's why I added my own observer implementation.

The code is written in TypeScript. Call the TypeScript transpiler first to get executable JavaScript:

```
$ tsc
```

The Demo Component

This Web Component in Listing 8-5 is just to demo the usage. It's a simple counter that can increase and decrease values.

Listing 8-5. Demo Component (chapter8/store/component.ts)

```
import { store, counterStoreType } from './store.js';

export class MainComponent extends HTMLElement {
  constructor() {
    super();
    store.subscribe('value', (state: counterStoreType): void => {
      const result = this.querySelector('[data-result]');
      result.textContent = state.value.toString();
    });
  }

  connectedCallback() {
    this.render();
  }
```

```
  render() {
    this.innerHTML = `
    <button data-action="INC" data-payload="1">Increment 1</button>
    <button data-action="INC" data-payload="5">Increment 5</button>
    <button data-action="DEC" data-payload="1">Decrement 1</button>
    <button data-action="DEC" data-payload="5">Decrement 5</button>
    <div data-result>0</div>
    `;
    this.querySelectorAll('button').forEach((btn) => {
      btn.addEventListener('click', (e) => this.invokeAction(e));
    });
  }

  invokeAction(e: Event) {
    const action = (e.target as HTMLElement).dataset.action;
    const payload = (e.target as HTMLElement).dataset.payload;
    store.dispatch(action, payload);
  }
}

customElements.define('app-main', MainComponent);
```

An event handler is added for the buttons (line 26) that call a handler method (line 30). Here you use the dataset object that handles the HTML 5 data- attributes as properties. After you have the right values, you dispatch the action along with the payload to the store (line 33). As you can see, the component does not contain any business logic. It also knows nothing about the inner structure of the store. The store is global and static.

The component also monitors an item in the store called value. It makes use of a subscription assigned in the constructor (lines 7 to 10). Once a change appears, the value is written into the DOM.

In a shadowed component, use this.shadowRoot.querySelector to get the right root element.

All the component must know is that you have actions (INC, DEC) and these actions accept a numeric payload. Also the component must know the actual storage (value).

The Store

The store code starts with the definition of the actions. In a more complex scenario, this could include the payload definition. Also, an Action interface is often a good idea. Here I tried to make it as simple as possible. The definition just says, "Dear developer, this is what the application can handle." See Listing 8-6.

Listing 8-6. The Actions (chapter8/store/actions.ts)

```
export const INC = 'INC';
export const DEC = 'DEC';
```

The business logic is a pure function call. This can be some calculation or even a server call to retrieve data from a REST service. In case of that, make the reducers async. See Listing 8-7.

Listing 8-7. The Reducers (chapter8/store/reducer.ts)

```
export const counterReducer = {
  [INC]: (state: counterStoreType, payload: number):
Partial<counterStoreType> => {
    const value = +state.value + payload;
    return { value };
  },
  [DEC]: (state: counterStoreType, payload: number):
Partial<counterStoreType> => {
    const value = +state.value - payload;
    return { value };
  },
};
```

The reducer is called by applying an action, provided as key (line 2 and 7). It will also receive the current state in case you need it. The second parameter is the payload. Not all actions in an app need a payload, so either provide null or make the parameter optional. In this example, you need the payload for both actions. Lines 4 and 9 have

the actual logic, which is very simple here. Then the reducer returns an object with
the actual change. It's a common pattern that a reducer has no side effects: one action
changes one value. But sometimes it's necessary to change more than one, so technically
it's possible (hence the object; see lines 5 and 10).

The store (see Listing 8-8) consists of two parts. The Store class itself is a base for all
stores and independent of a concrete type. To make this feasible, you use a generic T.

Listing 8-8. The Store Class (chapter8/store/store.ts)

```
import { Observer, callBackType } from './observer.js';

type actionType = { [key: string]: any };
type reducerType<T> = {
  [key: string]: (state: T, payload: any) => Partial<T>;
};

export class Store<T extends {}> {
  private state: any;
  private resolver: Map<string, any> = new Map();
  private observer: Observer;

  constructor(private actions: actionType, private reducer: reducerType<T>,
  state: T) {
    this.observer = Observer.getInstance();
    this.state = new Proxy(state, {
      set: (target: any, property: string, value: any) => {
        target[property] = value;
        this.observer.publish(property, this.state);
        return true;
      },
    });
  }

  dispatch(action: string, payload: any) {
    if (!Object.keys(this.actions).some((a) => a === action)) {
      throw new Error('Unknown action called: ' + action);
    }
```

```
  const toCall = this.reducer[action];
  if (!toCall) {
    throw new Error('Reducer not found for action: ' + action);
  }
  const newState = toCall(this.state, payload);
  Object.assign(this.state, newState);
}

subscribe(storeProperty: keyof T & string, cb: callBackType): void {
  this.observer.subscribe(storeProperty, cb);
}
}
```

The store has a Proxy (line 20) to supervise the changes. Whenever the state object changes, the proxy calls the observer and publishes the changes to all subscribers (line 22). The trigger is the reducer that's called by the dispatch method. Once a component dispatches an action, the code looks to see if it's valid, and if there is a reducer, it's called (toCall, line 37).

As an idea, you might use the call method each JavaScript function object has internally and then replace this value with the state object. This way you could save the first reducer parameter. It's less code but a bit tricky to read, hence I avoid such refinements in the book examples.

After the reducer has done its work, the changes are applied to the store state. That's the only point where it's allowed to change the store (line 38). The Proxy is triggered implicitly after this call.

Now, you define your actual store. The store is an instance of the Store<T> class. First, you create an interface that defines the store structure. From that, you derive a type that helps TypeScript to understand how to deal with the store values. See Listing 8-9.

Listing 8-9. A Concrete Store (chapter8/store/store.ts)

```
export interface counterStore {
  value: number;
}
```

```
export type counterStoreType = counterStore;
```

```
const counterState: counterStoreType = { value: 0 };
```

```
export const store = new Store<counterStoreType>({ INC, DEC }, {
...counterReducer }, counterState);
```

The actual store instance (line 9) is the only piece you will work with later. It knows the actions, the reducers, and the state. You may wonder why the values are not provided as arrays. Using objects is better here because in a real-life application the store structure might be more complicated. Assume you want to hold a state per component. That's easy because you just create another instance of the store class and assign the few values you need. Now you have a global store (usually just one) and a local store (also just one component). The objects can now easily be merged to a single store.

Merging Stores

To merge, you create a new store object that has parts, actions, reducers, and states. If you put it into the store class, a merge method could look like Listing 8-10.

Listing 8-10. An Idea for a Store Merge Function

```
mergeStore<V>(store: Store<V>): Store<T & V> {
  for (const action of Object.entries(store['actions'])) {
    const [key, payload] = action;
    if (this.actions.get(key)) {
      throw new Error(`Action ${key} already exists`);
    }
    this.actions.set(key, payload);
  }
  for (const reducer of Object.entries(store['reducer'])) {
    const [key, func] = reducer;
```

```
  if (this.reducer[key]) {
    throw new Error(`Reducer for action ${key} already exists`);
  }
  this.reducer[key] = func as any;
}
return this as Store<any>;
}
```

The returned type is then a join of both types T & V (line 1). The current object is enhanced and the existing store object (type V) is no longer in use.

This is just a suggestion. Once you have figured out your usage scenarios, other implementations might be better.

The Observer

The Observer class creates the publish/subscribe pattern. It's a singleton (one instance for all) and it handles subscriptions on a per store value base. See Listing 8-11.

Listing 8-11. Observer Implementation (chapter8/store/observer.ts)

```
export type callBackType = (...args: any) => void;

/**
 * Implement a simple pub/sub pattern to
 * have component communication without attributes.
 * This class is Singleton, use getInstance to get the global obj.
 */
export class Observer {
  private topics: { [id: string]: callBackType[] } = {};
  private hOP: any;

  constructor(s: any) {
    if (s !== void 0) {
      throw new Error("Observer is Singleton, don't call the ctor");
    }
    this.hOP = this.topics.hasOwnProperty;
  }
```

```
private static _instance: Observer;

public static getInstance(): Observer {
  if (!Observer._instance) {
    Observer._instance = new Observer(void 0);
  }
  return Observer._instance;
}

subscribe(topic: string, listener: callBackType): { remove: () => void } {
  // Create the topic's object if not yet created
  if (!this.hOP.call(this.topics, topic)) {
    this.topics[topic] = [];
  }
  // Add the listener to queue
  const index = this.topics[topic].push(listener) - 1;
  const self = this;
  // Provide handle back for removal of topic
  return {
    remove() {
      delete self.topics[topic][index]; // kill handler
      self.topics[topic].splice(index, 1); // shrink array
    },
  };
}

publish(topic: string, info: any): void {
  // If the topic doesn't exist,
  // or there's no listeners in queue, just leave
  if (!this.hOP.call(this.topics, topic)) return;
  // Cycle through topics queue, fire!
  this.topics[topic].forEach((item) => {
    item.call(item, info);
  });
}
}
```

It has only two methods: `publish` and `subscribe`. The subscriber registers a callback (or many), hence it's an array of arrays. The publisher loops through all the callbacks and calls them.

Note the return value in line 37. This is to safely remove the subscriber. It's not used in the demo code, but if you combine the Flux store with the router code shown earlier in this chapter, the components may unload. In that case, the subscription is still valid and the publisher will fire (into nowhere). This will cause memory leaks and will eventually decrease the performance. If that's your scenario, just use the `disconnectedCallback` method in the component class to call the `remove` method returned by the subscriber.

Summary

This chapter covered the two major concepts for creating single-page applications: router and store. The router handles routes and exchanges components dynamically. The store is the single source of truth for an application and holds the state for such ephemeral components.

The demo implementations are simple yet powerful. They show that you usually won't need an additional library or a dependency to achieve these goals. In combination with Web Components it's now possible to handle the most complex applications in a professional way.

CHAPTER 9

Professional Components

To further reduce the amount of code for Web Components I suggest some smart enhancements. By using decorators you can make the code even easier to read. That's the power of TypeScript. All examples in this chapter are written in TypeScript.

Before you start reading this chapter, it's recommended to get familiar with *decorators* in JavaScript and TypeScript.

Smart Selectors

When you work with the DOM, you often need to use `querySelector` and `querySelectorAll`. Most of the dynamics of components are in these calls. This can lead to code blocks that are hard to read. Even more critical, these blocks are hard to maintain. If the view code changes, you must browse the code manually and change the selectors accordingly. It's time to invent a smart selector.

The Smart Selector Decorator

A decorator definition can be applied to a create a virtual property. First, the selection of a single element using a `@Select()` decorator is shown in Listing 9-1.

Listing 9-1. The Smart Selector Decorator (chapter9/smart/single.ts)

```
export function Select(selector: string) {
  return function (target: any, prop: string) {
    Object.defineProperty(target, prop, {
      get: () => {
          this.querySelector(selector);
      }
```

J. Krause, *Developing Web Components with TypeScript*, https://doi.org/10.1007/978-1-4842-6840-7_9

```
      },
      enumerable: false,
      configurable: false
    });
  };
}
```

The selection of several elements using a @SelectAll() decorator is shown in Listing 9-2.

Listing 9-2. The Smart Selector Decorator (chapter9/smart/all.ts)

```
export function SelectAll(selector: string) {
  return function (target: any, prop: string) {
    Object.defineProperty(target, prop, {
      get: () => {
          this.querySelectorAll(selector);
        }
      },
      enumerable: false,
      configurable: false
    });
  };
}
```

Now, in a component you use the decorator like this:

```
@Select('button#start') btn: HTMLButtonElement;
```

The advantage is that the selector appears exactly once, regardless of how often you use the referenced element.

How Does It Work?

The decorator is executed after the component is instantiated. It's set on a property and the call includes the property name. Because common properties in JavaScript do not have any restrictions, the decorator function replaces the property with a new variant of the same name. This new property has multiple settings:

- The property is not changeable (`configurable: false`).

- The property is not enumerable. This means if you iterate over all properties with a `for of` loop, it's invisible. Note that this doesn't change its ability to be directly accessible.

- The property is read-only. It has only a getter and here you call the `querySelectorAll` or `querySelector` method.

You could also do this another way, using a second parameter and combining the calls to `querySelectorAll` and `querySelector` into one decorator. The example should give you just an idea what decorators are for and how powerful such a little piece of code can be.

Data Binding

Almost all of the major frameworks provide data binding. In fact, the manufacturers of these frameworks often try to tell everybody that the binding is one of the core features. It's quite helpful and it means you can avoid writing a lot of code, indeed. Out of the box, Web Components don't have full support for data binding. Hence, you need to write a bit of code to get a similar behavior.

Why Data Binding?

Data binding is a way to bind element properties to pure code objects. Imagine a form with some text boxes. The application pulls some data from a REST service and you have to write, property by property, all the values into the text boxes. This means first selecting the right element, figuring out the property to use, and writing the value into it. If something must be changed, element names, property names, data types, or whatever, there are several lines of code that need to be adjusted. Sounds like a lot of work and a good source for errors. And it is the weak part of Web Components, indeed.

Implementing Data Binding

But the framework manufacturers are no magicians and the code they use internally is not so hard to understand. It's impossible to do something similar with plain TypeScript. So, let's look at how it could work.

143

First, to detect changes of object data, you can use a `Proxy` object. It is native ECMAScript2015 and all modern browsers offer full support. A proxy monitors all properties and calls a callback function when a change occurred. You can now look up some sort of definition, select the appropriate target element (the one bound to), and write the value into the right property.

Second, the reverse way is a little more effort. Changes to the DOM can be monitored, but changes to element properties will fire events. This means you need to add events to any bound element and monitor them. An additional challenge is to avoid backfire. If you write the value received by an event handler back into the proxied object, the proxy will fire the binding and access the element. You can assume that the element will not fire the event again in case of input elements that are smart enough to understand a real change, but some simple events might not handle this as expected. In extreme situations, this results in a loop.

As you can see, there is a lot to consider. Let's take a look into a simplified approach. This is a component that includes all the binding code for the sake of simplicity (in a real project, you would extract this part into a separate class). Let's go through the code step by step.

To have support for types in the editor, it's recommended to use a view model. Technically it's a simple class:

```
class InputViewModel {
  field: string = '';
}
```

The component has a text box (input element), an output element (span), and a button to show how to change a value programmatically. All these parts are defined in the `connectedCallback` method. In the constructor, the view model is instantiated as a proxy (line 6). Listing 9-3 shows the complete code.

Listing 9-3. A Component with Data Binding (chapter9/binding/component.ts)

```
class BindableComponent extends HTMLElement {
  model: Record<string, any>;

  constructor() {
    super();
    this.model = new Proxy(new InputViewModel(), {
      get: (target: any, prop: string, receiver: any) => {
```

```
      return target[prop];
    },
    set: (target: any, prop: string, val: any, rec: any) => {
      target[prop] = val;
      const elements = this.querySelectorAll<any>('[data-bind]');
      elements.forEach((element) => {
        const attribute = element.dataset.bind;
        const [field, property] = attribute.split(':', 2);
        if (element[property] !== target[field]) {
          element[property] = target[field];
        }
      });
      return true;
    },
  });
}

reset() {
  this.model.field = '';
}

connectedCallback() {
  this.innerHTML = `
    <form>
      <label>Input Field:</label>
      <input type="text" data-bind="field:value:input" />
      <hr />
      <button type="button">Reset Field</button>
      <hr />
      <div>
        You typed the following text:
        <span data-bind="field:textContent" />
      </div>
    </form>
  `;
  const elements = this.querySelectorAll<HTMLElement>('[data-bind]');
```

```
  elements.forEach((element) => {
    const attribute = element.dataset.bind;
    const [field, property, event] = attribute.split(':', 3);
    if (event) {
      element.addEventListener(event, (e: Event) => {
        this.model[field] = (e.target as any)[property];
      });
    }
  });
  this.querySelector('button').addEventListener('click', this.reset.
  bind(this));
  }
}

customElements.define('app-bindable', BindableComponent);
```

To trigger the binder, you need a binding configuration. To stay HTML-compliant, use data- attributes. In the attribute, you define two or three distinct values: model Property:element property:event name. The third value, the event, is optional. Some elements such as the output <span> do not fire events, obviously. The code is split into two parts, as per the thoughts in the beginning of this section.

The proxy intercepts the setter path and reacts to changes in the view model. It looks for bindable elements, extracts the binding instructions into the fields field and property, and sets the values accordingly.

The event handler is added once after the connectedCallback has written the DOM. The same strategy is used here. First, the binding instructions are extracted, the handler is attached accordingly, and the received value (determined by the binding instruction) is written into the model. The proxy checks for changes to avoid the backfire.

The button is just to demonstrate the programmatic change and how the value is shown immediately on the screen. Please note the bind call here that is required to set the component itself as this in the buttons click event handler. Alternatively, you can use a complete function call like this (the lambda expression prevents the handler from changing this):

```
() => this.reset();
```

Discussion

Of course, all this is extremely simple. It's works very well, too. One possible improvement is to cache the retrieving of bindable elements. In the current code, the call `querySelectorAll` happens on each value change. In complex applications, this could take too much time.

The handling of types is not optimal, though. The model is of type `InputViewModel`, but the definition type is `Record<string, any>`. This is currently a requirement because the access to the model itself is dynamically using the `instance[property]` syntax. It works perfectly in JavaScript, but TypeScript doesn't understand the intention and complains about the weak type usage. Here a generic could help. On the other hand, if you extract the code and write a generic class that handles the bindings, it doesn't matter anymore because the actual type is an abstract one anyway.

The definition in the `data-bind` attributes is obviously not type safe, too. An editor extension could handle this (this happens with Angular, where the editors don't understand the binding too, but for Angular editor extensions exist). To become type safe and avoid the need for additional editor support, you need a template language that has both common editor support and the ability to deal with TypeScript natively. It's beyond the scope of this section, but this exists for sure. See more about this in the section about *template engines* further below in this chapter.

I hope you can see that the effort to have bidirectional data binding is not that huge. The actual code that's part of the binding stuff is less than 20 lines. It's a bit tricky in all the details, but apart from being not entirely trivial it's not worth it to add a complete framework with hundreds of kilobytes of code for such a simple thing. Write your own thin library or use an existing one that provides just this. It's mostly enough.

Forms and Validation

The same strategy can be used for validation. The idea here is to have validation information somewhere and use the binding code to handle any reaction to validation activity. This means once a value changes, a callback is triggered to check the actual value against some rule (required, maxlength, or a pattern, for instance). If that happens, the outcome is usually true or false. Now use the binding code to set an element's visibility; the error message appears or disappears. It's a bit more effort because you need to handle the form's entire state. This includes the first appearance (called pristine) where you won't want to have all error messages to appear immediately. You need to handle the dirty state (values changed) and of course the validation state (valid/invalid).

A good approach is the usage of decorators. This could look like the following code snippet:

```
class InputViewModel {
  @Required()
  field: string = '';
}
```

All the @Required decorator needs to do is to create a hidden property that stores the validation instruction:

```
class InputViewModel {
  field: string = '';

  _field_required_active = true;
  _field_required_message = 'Some custom error message';
  _field_required_valid = (value: any) => {
    return !!value;
  };
}
```

The validation code would now, when handling the property field, look for these magic properties, and if they exist, handle them accordingly.

Sketching a Solution

A working example will show the effective effort you need to implement this idea. It is, of course, far from complete; the code is reduced to the bare minimum to get it working. In fact, it lacks all error checking and is in no way universal. But more validation options, exporting the code base to external classes, and error checking are all just refinements and they don't change the basic strategy at all.

First, let's have a look at the complete example. It consists of three parts:

- The decorator definition for a supposed Required decorator

- A view model class that's using it

- An example component with the glue code to get the decorator working

The Required Decorator

This decorator has just one purpose: add a few hidden properties to the model class. It looks like the code in Listing 9-4.

Listing 9-4. Simple Component (chapter9/validation/component.ts)

```
function Required() {
  function RequiredDecorator(target: any, property: string) {
    Object.defineProperties(target, {
      [`__req__${property}__`]: {
        value: true,
        writable: false,
        enumerable: false,
        configurable: false
      },
      [`__req__${property}__val__`]: {
        get: function () {
          return !!this[property];
        },
        enumerable: false,
        configurable: false
      },
      [`__req__${property}__msg__`]: {
        value: `The field ${property} is required.`,
        enumerable: false,
        configurable: false
      }
    });
  }
  return RequiredDecorator;
}
```

The name is up to you; the function determines how the decorator is named. More important is the returned function `RequiredDecorator`, where the name is not relevant but its signature makes it work. The structure and type of parameters determines that this decorator can be placed on a property. That's exactly what you want to do.

You define three distinct properties, all with enumerable: false. This way you can loop over the "real" properties without being inferred by the special ones. The names are dynamic to make them dependent on the concrete property the decorator refers to.

The first __req__${property}__ is just a marker. It always returns true. You use it as a trigger before you investigate the object further. The second is the actual validation logic. It looks up the property and returns true if valid. Note that the object this refers to the whole view model, not just the current property. That's quite helpful, as you can use it to compare properties in more complex scenarios. The third is an error message. It's hard-coded here but a more dynamic approach would be easy to use. You can add any number of parameters to this decorator to deliver a message, for example:

```
function Required(message: string) {
  function RequiredDecorator(target: any, property: string) {
    // omitted for brevity
    Object.defineProperties(target, {
      [`__req__${property}__msg__`]: {
        value: message || `The field ${property} is required.`
      }
    });
  }
  return RequiredDecorator;
}
```

Here the static text is just a fallback and the developer can override the message.

In case you wonder how the code refers to the parameters later at runtime, have a look at the subject "closures." Closures keep a function closed and the parameters' values encapsulated so they are still accessible later. It's a powerful technique of pure JavaScript.

The View Model

Now, once you have the decorator, you can use it on a model class like the one shown in Listing 9-5.

Listing 9-5. Simple Component (chapter9/validation/component.ts)

```
class ValidationViewModel {
  @Required()
  city: string = '';
  @Required()
  street: string = '';
}
```

The decorators are "stackable," which means you can use multiple ones on the same property. They execute in the order of definition:

```
@Required()
@Maxlength(100)
city: string = '';
```

In this code snippet, the @Required decorator will be called first, the @MaxLength one last.

The Example Component

Finally, here's the component that uses this model. Apart from the very common definition, the code that activates the validation is moved to the method bindValidation. See Listing 9-6.

Listing 9-6. Simple Component (chapter9/validation/component.ts)

```
class ValidationDemoComponent extends HTMLElement {

  model: ValidationViewModel & Record<string, any>;

  constructor() {
    super();
    this.model = new ValidationViewModel();
  }

  connectedCallback() {
    this.innerHTML = `
      <form>
        <div>
```

```
      <label>City:</label>
      <input type="text" data-val="city:Required" />
      <span data-err="city:Required" />
    </div>
    <div>
      <label>Street:</label>
      <input type="text" data-val="street:Required" />
      <span data-err="street:Required" />
    </div>
    <hr />
    <button type="button">Validate</button>
  </form>
`;
  this.bindValidation();
}

bindValidation() {
  Object.keys(this.model).forEach(property => {
    // loop enhanced properties, look for bind/val instructions
    if (this.model[`__req__${property}__`]) {
      const fieldSelector = `[data-val="${property}:Required"]`;
      const f = this.querySelector(fieldSelector);
      const msgSelector = `[data-err="${property}:Required"]`;
      const m = this.querySelector(msgSelector);
      f.addEventListener('input', (e) => {
        const value = (e.target as HTMLInputElement).value;
        this.model[property] = value;
        const v = this.model[`__req__${property}__val__`];
        if (!v) {
          // field invalid
          const msg = this.model[`__req__${property}__msg__`]
          m.textContent = msg;
        } else {
          m.textContent = null;
        }
      });
```

```
    }
  });
  }
}
customElements.define('app-validator', ValidationDemoComponent);
```

The code loops over the model's properties. The hidden properties from the decorator are skipped. You can still access these hidden properties by using the [ ] named property syntax. To stop the TypeScript transpiler complaining about such access, there are two options. You can either allow this globally in the settings of tsconfig.json (allowAny option). Of you can extend the model type to allow index access like this:

```
model: ValidationViewModel & Record<string, any>;
```

This is definitely the better option. Using this definition you can now safely look for the trigger this.model[__req__${property}__], pull the related fields, and if they exist, add the required action. In this example, the selectors are data-val for any element that has to be validated and data-err for any element that can expose an error message to the user. The event listener watches the user typing, and once the validation property returns false, the message appears. If everything is fine, the message disappears. Once the form loads initially, the message is invisible.

Again, even if this code works perfectly well, it's extremely reduced to just explain the concept. It shows that there is not so much magic behind huge frameworks, just a smart usage of the features of JavaScript and a clever approach to express this in TypeScript.

UI-less Components

Sometimes you want to provide functionality a view developer can use, but the function does not create any UI actually. UI-less components offer a more markup-first approach to an application.

Directives

This is a further development of the UI-less components described in the last section. It's not very well supported on the API level, hence the solution isn't very attractive. Nonetheless it's worth having a look at the strategic part. See Listing 9-7.

Listing 9-7. UI-less Components (chapter9/directive/component.ts)

```
class DirectiveDemo extends HTMLElement {
  connectedCallback() {
    this.parentElement.dataset.items = JSON.stringify([1, 2, 3]);
  }
}
class DirectiveDemoComponent extends HTMLElement {
  connectedCallback() {
    this.appendChild(document.createElement('app-directive-demo'));
    this.innerHTML = `
      <div>${this.dataset.items}</div>
    `;
  }
}
customElements.define('app-directive-demo', DirectiveDemo);
customElements.define('app-directive', DirectiveDemoComponent);
```

The first definition, `DirectiveDemo`, is UI-less and just retrieves some static data. It's added in the second component to get it working (`DirectiveDemoComponent`). The API call to `appendChild` is necessary to invoke the callback before the one of the hosting components is completed; otherwise the dataset would return `undefined`. Now you have it as a component and can use it in all other components without worrying about references or implementation details. Also, you can add attributes for configuration.

Discussion

This example shows that Web Components still lack a lot of common features provided by frameworks. The implementation effort depends on what you are trying to achieve. In regard to UI-less components, I suggest not using this technique and moving the code to a Flux store, as shown in Chapter 8, or using a publish/subscribe pattern directly. If you encapsulate the code in another layer of indirection, it could be easier to use, but this is nothing you can achieve with just a few lines of code. The library **@nyaf** documented in the Appendix has a full implementation for attribute-based directives. It's effectively less than one kilobyte of code, so it's not a real burden for a project, but the sheer amount of boilerplate code is significant if you think in terms of just a few components.

Template Engines

The first question about this should always be, "Do I really need this?" If you would like to simplify the process of view creation, use any of the templating engines for JavaScript. With the powerful and convenient code style, web developers around the world have a chance to create real masterpieces.

Plugins have expanded beyond the comprehension of an average developer, and we also saw, and highly anticipated, the release of ECMAScript 6, the new JavaScript standard. Frankly, ES6 was already on the way; it just needed to be finalized. Make sure to check out the full spec if you haven't done so already. ECMAScript 6 improvements include better syntax for classes, along with new methods for strings, arrays, promises, maps, and sets.

We keep seeing huge growth with frameworks such as Meteor, Angular, and React that have also made their way into the global JavaScript ecosphere. Needless to say, there have been some truly revolutionary additions to an already established system of development.

A templating engine is basically a way for developers to interpolate strings effectively. If you are a heavy front-end JavaScript developer, using a templating engine will save you countless hours of unnecessary work. And because of the vast array of templating engines available today, it can be tough to make the right choice at the right time. So let's take a look at the most popular and dubbed best (by the community) templating engines for JavaScript today.

Mustache

Mustache is one of the most widely known templating systems. It works for a number of programming languages, including JavaScript, Node.js, PHP, and many others. Because Mustache is a logic-less templating engine, it can be literally used for any kind of development work. It works by expanding tags in a template using values provided in a hash or object. The term "logic-less" comes from the fact that Mustache works purely by using tags. All values are set and executed according to tags, so you end up saving yourself hours of "nasty" development work. Take a strategic shortcut, if you will.

Somehow Mustache is the mother of all template engines, as it's the original implementation of the curly braces (hence the name) syntax:

```
The person {{person}} is
shown.
{{#person}}
Never shown!
{{/person}}
```

The curly braces are the trigger to switch to the dynamic part, where additional functions may follow or just a replacement with variables.

Handlebars

Handlebars is a close successor to Mustache with the ability to swap out tags where necessary. The only difference is that Handlebars is more focused on helping developers create semantic templates, without all of the confusion and time consumption. You can easily try out Handlebars yourself (there's also an option to try Mustache on the same page) and decide whether this is the type of templating engine you're looking for. Last but not least, Handlebars was set up to work flawlessly in any ECMAScript 3 environment. In other words, Handlebars works with Node.js, Chrome, Firefox, Safari, and others. The syntax is almost the same as for Mustache.

jQuery Templating

jQuery Templating provides all the necessary features you are looking for in a templating engine for JavaScript. It is a tool that you will have no trouble using. Not only that, it is fast, uses valid HTML5, and utilizes only pure HTML for templates. On the other hand, you can also pick up a jQuery object as the template. You can quickly populate the templates by simply calling `jQuery.loadTemplate`. jQuery Templating also ensures a clean final product, meaning the data will flow smoothly. Head over to the official website of jQuery Templating to learn how it works and how to apply it and make a difference.

The basic idea is more HTML-driven, using the dataset properties:

```
<div data-template-bind='[
    {"attribute": "content", "value": "post"},
    {"attribute": "data-date", "value": "date"},
    {"attribute": "data-author", "value": "author"}
    ]'>
</div>
```

This is a so-called markup-first approach, where you write pure HTML and enhance it according to your needs.

Lit Element (lit-html)

Lit Element is part of the Polymer project, one of the first (and still best) Web Component thin libraries. Here the JavaScript part provides the initial call and a function is used to activate the templating engine:

```
html`<p>Hello, ${this.name}!</p>`
```

The single quotes are backticks, a pure JavaScript function. The crucial part is the way the function named html is called. Instead of using a regular function call with round brackets, this call writes the string directly after the function name. Because the backticks are in fact string interpolations, the JavaScript engine treats this syntax as a special function call. The receiving function does not get a string; instead, it receives an array of fragments that consists of the pure text parts and the interpolation part (${…}). This way the engine can replace and process the dynamic parts very easily.

The biggest advantage is speed. The engine is mostly pure JavaScript, does not need much template code, and the replacements happen on a very basic level.

JSX/TSX

One of the best choices is JSX (if you use TypeScript, it's called TSX, but it's exactly the same syntax). It was invented by Facebook for its famous UI library React. The idea is fundamentally different from all other templating engines. While in all other engines the HTML markup is a first class citizen and the dynamic part, the scripting stuff, is added by some magic syntax, JSX is primarily JavaScript. The script part is now the first class citizen and the HTML part is embedded when needed. This part, the markup, is not forwarded to the browser but parsed and replaced by JavaScript. Technically, each element is transformed into a function call. These chains of function calls return HTML later.

This sounds complicated and the code behind is far from trivial. But it has a real advantage. You can code in your template and do almost everything by just using JavaScript (or TypeScript). So, instead of learning some new syntax with all the typical rough edges, you work with what you already know perfectly well.

But the best thing about JSX is that any modern editor can handle it without additional plug-ins or extensions. And those that can't have an extension for sure. The TypeScript transpiler understands JSX very well and even here you don't need to add anything. Just tell `tsconfig.json` that you use JSX.

Here's an example to give you an impression:

```
const div = <div class='alert'>Content</div>;
```

This is simple yet powerful, because you handle the HTML part (note that there are no braces or quotes here) just like code. In fact, it is code at runtime (after transpiling).

But how does this work? The transpiler replaces the code with simple functions calls:

```
const div = createElement('div', { class: 'alert' }, 'Content');
```

That's it. What a typical library provides is the code that makes `createElement` working. However, it looks like this is totally up to the library author. You can deduce from this that there is absolutely no relation to React anymore. React is just one, very good and complete, implementation of such a library.

Making Your Own Using JSX

At first glance, this sounds simply crazy. The library React where JSX was used the first time is complex and well developed. Nothing you can reproduce easily. But you won't need all of React, and stripping it down to the bare templating part is astonishingly easy.

Activating JSX

To activate JSX, you use the TypeScript transpiler. There are other options, such as Babel, for using Pure ES2015 and beyond, but TypeScript is definitely the most flexible one. The configuration file tsconfig.json has two settings you actually need:

- "jsx": This should be set to "react".

- "reactNamespace": This should be the name of your implementation.

Don't worry about the "react" setting. It has nothing to do with React. You just want to mimic its behavior. The name of the namespace is the implementation. Usually it's *JSX*, but any name will do it. Let's keep the default for now. See Listing 9-8.

Listing 9-8. Section of tsconfig.json for JSX

```
"jsx": "react",
"reactNamespace": "JSX",
"noImplicitAny": false
```

The setting noImplicitAny: false is required because the original implementation that's made to support React requires a special interface that defines all existing HTML elements. It's kind of a syntax checker by simply using TypeScript types. That's sort of an effort to create such checker code. The implementation shown here has no such interface and hence the transpiler assumes the return type is any. To support this kind of simplification, you need to allow any as a type for all unknown type declarations. It's not really a culprit, but because of the global setting it reduces the strictness of the type system.

Implementing JSX

The transpiler is quite simple. It replaces all the JSX calls with a function called createElement. The createElement function has three parameters:

- The element's name

- An object with all attributes

- An object that provides the element's children

The third parameter is usually again a call to createElement, where the cycle continues down the tree of elements.

The root element is the one you touch in your component. What the method returns is up to you. If you plan to assign the rendered template to innerHTML, then the return type is string. If you deal with DOM operations, an instance of Node or even HTMLElement is sufficient.

Listing 9-9 shows an easy example that handles just pure HTML.

Listing 9-9. Simple JSX Implementation

```
const JSX = {
  createElement(name: string,
                props: { [id: string]: any },
              ...content: any[]): string {
    content = [].concat.apply([], content);
    const flat = function (arr1: string[]): string[] {
      return arr1.reduce((acc, val) =>
        (Array.isArray(val)
          ?
          acc.concat(flat(val))
          :
          acc.concat(val)), []);
    };
    props = props || {};
    let ifStore = true;
    let isRepeater = false;
    const styleStore: { [rule: string]: string } = {};
    let propsstr =
      Object.keys(props)
        .map(key => {
          const value = props[key];
        })
        .join(' ') || '';
```

```
  if (!name) {
    // support for   fake container tag
    return `${flat(content).join('')}`;
  }
  return (
    `<${name}${propsstr ? ' ' : ''}${propsstr}>` +
    flat(content).join('') +
    `</${name}>`);
  }
};
export default JSX;
```

Why all this? Say you write such a piece in your script because you need some HTML:

```
const div = <div class="alert">Some Content</div>;
```

This is pure JSX, but neither JavaScript nor the browser can read this. The transpiler is doing you a favor and transforms this to function calls:

```
const div = JSX.createElement(
  'div',
  { 'class': 'alert' },
  'Some Content');
```

You have previously defined that a string value is sufficient in your app. Hence the function call will produce something like this:

```
const div = <div class="alert">Some Content</div>;
```

So, why not write this directly? Of course this will work. But JSX is very well-supported by editors, and the way you wrote it in the first example the editor would produce some nice syntax highlighting, point to common mistakes, and start understanding proper HTML semantics. That's a big advantage. Moreover, if you find some HTML, you just copy and paste it into your template as is. If the snippets grow, just use multiple lines. Don't worry about using quotes with concatenation or backticks or whatever; this is no longer relevant. JSX makes no differentiation between script code and HTML.

The best thing comes next. What if you want to embed dynamic parts? Here you can use the curly braces shown earlier in this chapter. Just use single braces where code access is needed:

```
const div = <div class="alert">{this.content}</div>;
```

The final code is not just a replacement, it is the original code and appears like this:

```
const div = JSX.createElement(
  'div',
  { 'class': 'alert' },
  this.content);
```

This means the code is pure JavaScript, with no restriction at all. It just needs to fit in as a parameter. That said, you can use the ternary operator `expression ? true : false`, but you can't use keywords such as `if` or `while`.

Extending the Syntax

Because you're now in the position of controlling the render process, it's easy to introduce additional templating features. I won't go into much detail here. Adding support for a new template language on top of JSX would contradict the simplicity of the whole approach. But a few tweaks could be helpful. Let's assume that in your code the usage of conditional rendering happens very often:

```
const div = show ? <div class="alert">Some Content</div> : null;
```

In bigger components this could lead to code blocks that become hard to read and heavily fragmented. Isn't it easier to read something like this?

```
const div = <div class="alert" if={show}>Some Content</div>;
```

However, if there is no valid HTML attribute and it's exactly the kind of dynamic, that's the reason for all the templates engines.

Summary

In this chapter, I covered some professional coding styles and advanced subjects. Depending on your project and the concrete requirements, this can guide you through the obstacles of huge applications or particular challenges. The examples include the usage of decorators, ideas to implement data binding, and a strategy to add an abstract validation layer. Last, but not least, a custom implementation of the famous JSX templating style was shown.

APPENDIX A

Introducing @nyaf

The name @nyaf is an acronym for "Not Yet Another Framework." It is, in fact, an entirely new concept of a web development support library, a so-called "thin library."

It's simple, has a flat learning curve, and doesn't need any special tools. Keep your tool chain, get the power. It can replace all the complex stuff such as React or Angular entirely, indeed.

The package has no dependencies! It's pure HTML 5 DOM API and ES 2015 Code. Super small, super smart, super powerful.

Write front-end apps without the hassle of a complex framework, use the full power of HTML 5, keep a component-based style.

Elevator Pitch

Since the amazing impact of jQuery in 2006 we have seen an uncountable number of JavaScript frameworks. Some good, some nice, a few excellent. Each time has its leading frameworks and an audience that loves them. The love comes from the simple properties. It should save time compared with programming on a more basic level. It should give stability and reliability to your apps where things in the browser's internal parts get messy. And it should add another layer of indirection to make things smooth and good looking, nicely maintainable, and well-architected.

But over time, frameworks get older. And they can't change and evolve because they have a broad audience and hundreds or thousands of projects relying on them. The manufacturer can't break everything to go to the next step. The programmers get stuck.

© Jörg Krause 2021
J. Krause, *Developing Web Components with TypeScript*, https://doi.org/10.1007/978-1-4842-6840-7

And the world of browser programming keeps evolving dramatically. Meanwhile, we have an amazingly powerful native API in HTML 5.

One of the most important innovations in browser development is Web Components. The API is easy to learn, the support is complete for all modern browsers, and the implementation is stable. At the same time, the programming language TypeScript has come along with a powerful toolset.

It's time for the next step. Take the leading tools and create an easy-to-use library that covers the hard stuff and is where the native API is almost the best. This is the core idea behind @nyaf.

Parts

The library comes in three parts:

- A core library that handles Web Components the easy way, provides a router for single-page apps, and adds a nice template language

- A forms library that handles data binding and decorator-based validation

- A store library that gives your app a state engine using the common Flux architecture style

Everything else is simple HTML 5 API, without any restrictions. You can add CSS, other libraries, or your own stuff at almost any position.

Additionally, there is a small CLI for easy setup and component creation.

Project Configuration with TypeScript

A @nyaf application consists of

1. An entry file for registering components, typically called `main.ts`

2. At least one root component

3. The `index.html` file the browser loads first

4. The configuration for TypeScript, `tsconfig.json`

5. The packer/builder setup

The best choice for a packer is probably WebPack. In this case, a `webpack.config.js` file is recommended.

The Entry File

The recommended folder structure looks like this:

```
|
\--\src
|   |-- index.html
|   |-- main.ts
|   \-- \components
|   |                 |
|   |                 \-- main.component.tsx
|   |
|   \-- \assets
|
|-- webpack.config.js
|-- tsconfig.json
```

The application starts with the code in `main.ts` and the basics structure looks like Figure A-1.

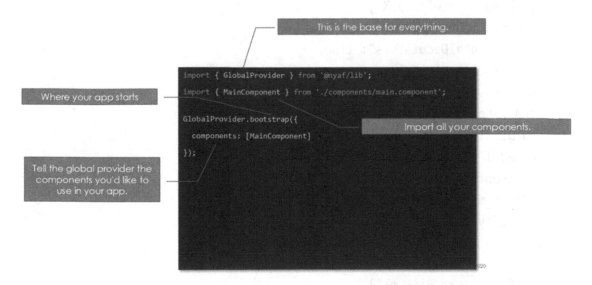

Figure A-1. *Entry file*

TypeScript Configuration

The TypeScript configuration is typical, but two things are crucial to know:

1. You need to compile with the target "es2015" (minimum). ES 5 is explicitly not supported anymore.

2. The template language is a variety of JSX, so the settings "jsx" and "reactNamespace" are required.

@nyaf does not use React, has no relation to React, and has almost nothing in common with it. The setting just tricks the compiler to transpile the templates.

```
{
  "compilerOptions": {
    "target": "es2015",
    "module": "commonjs",
    "moduleResolution": "node",
    "resolveJsonModule": true,
    "sourceMap": true,
    "lib": ["es2018", "es5", "dom"],
    "jsx": "react",
    "reactNamespace": "JSX",
    "declaration": false,
    "experimentalDecorators": true,
    "noImplicitAny": false,
    "suppressImplicitAnyIndexErrors": true,
    "removeComments": false,
    "outDir": "out-tsc",
    "baseUrl": "./src",
    "typeRoots": [
      "node_modules/@types",
      "src/types"
    ]
  },
  "files": ["./src/main.ts"]
}
```

First, the target must be "es2015" or higher. There are some native features used here that don't have polyfills. The recommended template language is JSX (or in TypeScript it's called TSX). It's not enforced, so you can also use pure string templates, but all examples in this documentation and the snippets shown online use JSX. Hence the following settings are highly recommended:

- "jsx": "react" activates JSX although we don't use React
- "reactNamespace": "JSX" is the name of the support class in @nyaf (this **is** mandatory if JSX is used)

All other settings follow the common requirements of a typical TypeScript application.

WebPack Configuration

WebPack is the recommended packer tool, but you can use any other if you like. There is no dependency.

A typical configuration will look like this:

```
const dev = process.env.NODE_ENV === 'dev';
const path = require('path');
const HtmlWebpackPlugin = require('html-webpack-plugin');

// Main entry point
const indexConfig = {
  template: './src/index.html',
  inject: 'body',
  baseHref: './'
};

const webpackConfig = {
  mode: 'development',
  // How source maps are generated : style of source mapping
  devtool: dev ? 'eval-cheap-module-source-map' : false,
  // Development server configuration
```

```
devServer: {
  historyApiFallback: true,
  contentBase: path.join(__dirname, 'dist'),
  compress: true,
  port: 9000
},
// Where webpack looks to start building the bundle
entry: {
  'app': './src/main.ts' // App entry point
},
// How the different types of modules within
// a project will be treated
module: {
  rules: [
    { test: /\.ts|\.tsx$/ , loader: 'ts-loader' },
    // All files with a '.scss' extension
    // will be handled by sass-loader
    {
      test: /\.(scss)$/ ,
      use: [
        'style-loader',
        'css-loader',
        'sass-loader'
      ]
    },
    {
      test: /\.css$/,
      use: ['style-loader', 'css-loader']
    },
    {
      test: /\.(png|jpeg)$/ ,
      loader: 'url-loader?limit=8192'},
    {
      test: /\.(woff|woff2)$/ ,
      loader: 'file-loader'
```

```
      }
    ]
  },
  // Configure how modules are resolved
  resolve: {
    extensions: ['.ts', '.tsx', '.js', '.scss']
  },
  // How and where webpack should output
  // bundles, assets and anything else
  output: {
    path: path.resolve('./dist'),
    filename: '[name].js'
  },
  // Customize the webpack build process with additional plugins
  plugins: [
    new HtmlWebpackPlugin(indexConfig)
  ]
};

// Export the config
module.exports = webpackConfig;
```

See the comments inline for important explanations. Apart from this, the configuration has no special settings and follows the common rules of a typical WebPack setup.

Project Configuration with Babel

If you don't want to use TypeScript, you can still get the full power of @nyaf. All features that the package requires are provided by ES2017 and above. The recommended tool to set up a package for ES2015 any modern browser supports is Babel.

This section describes the setup and usage with pure ECMAScript.

Setting Up the Environment

If you use Visual Studio Code, it's recommended to tell the editor the specific features you use, especially decorators. To do so, add a file named `jsconfig.json` in the project root and add this content:

```
{
  "compilerOptions": {
    "baseUrl": "./src",
    "target": "es6",
    "module": "commonjs",
    "experimentalDecorators": true
  },
  "include": ["src/**/*"]
}
```

This assumes your sources are in the folder `./src`. Adjust the settings according to your needs.

Project Dependencies

Next, add the following dependencies to your project's `package.json`. This is the current Babel 7 setup.

```
"dependencies": {
    "@nyaf/forms": "^0.6.1",
    "@nyaf/lib": "^0.6.1",
    "@nyaf/store": "^0.6.1",
    "babel-loader": "^8.1.0"
  },
  "devDependencies": {
    "@babel/core": "^7.11.6",
    "@babel/plugin-proposal-decorators": "^7.10.5",
    "@babel/preset-env": "^7.11.5",
    "@babel/preset-react": "^7.10.4",
    "html-webpack-plugin": "^4.4.1",
    "webpack-cli": "^3.3.12",
```

```
    "webpack": "^4.44.1",
    "webpack-dev-server": "^3.11.0"
}
```

This setup allows the compilation and packaging with WebPack, but the transformation invoked from WebPack is based on the Babel plug-ins.

Configuring Babel

Next, configure Babel to support the features @nyaf needs. This is primarily the JSX namespaces, which are different from React. It's similar to the procedure described for TypeScript. However, the settings look a bit different.

You can use either .babelrc or the settings in package.json. The following example shows the settings in package.json (on the root level).

```
"babel": {
    "presets": [
      "@babel/preset-env",
      [
        "@babel/preset-react", {
          "runtime": "classic",
          "pragma": "JSX.createElement",
          "pragmaFrag": "null"
        }
      ]
    ],
    "plugins": [
      [
        "@babel/plugin-proposal-decorators",
        {
          "legacy": true
        }
      ]
    ]
  }
```

The core settings you need are `preset-react` and `plugin-proposal-decorators`. The first activates the compilation for the *JSX* namespace `JSX.createElement`. This is the exact and complete call to the @nyaf JSX module. The second parameter `pragmaFrag` is the support for the `<>` fragment syntax. In React, it's `React.fragment`. In @nyaf it's just nothing, as the JSX module treats missing element information as a fragment. To enforce this, just provide `null`.

The decorator support is provided by a plugin. Babel takes care to compile this using a polyfill so it runs on the selected ECMAScript version.

Configuring WebPack

The Babel transpiler can create a bundle, but putting it all together requires additional steps. The most powerful way (not always the easiest) is WebPack. The following `webpack.config.js` file is all you need to set up WebPack to create a bundle using Babel:

```js
const HtmlWebpackPlugin = require('html-webpack-plugin');

module.exports = {
  entry: './src/main.js',
  module: {
    rules: [
      {
        test: /\.(jsx?)$/,
        exclude: /node_modules/,
        use: ['babel-loader'],
      },
    ],
  },
  resolve: {
    extensions: ['*', '.js', '.jsx'],
  },
  output: {
    path: __dirname + '/dist',
    publicPath: '/',
    filename: 'bundle.js',
  },
```

```
devServer: {
    contentBase: './dist',
  },
  plugins: [
    new HtmlWebpackPlugin({
      inject: true,
      template: './src/index.html',
    }),
  ],
};
```

The entry point is the file main.js. All component files have the extension .jsx, so you need to resolve that extension, too. Apart from this, the babel-loader invokes the Babel transpiler and the settings, described above, apply here. The bundle is copied to the distribution folder dist and the bundle is added to the HTML file using the appropriate plugin.

Writing Components

The components look exactly like the ones using TypeScript, apart from missing types and generics. Let's assume you have this index.html:

```
<!DOCTYPE html>
<html lang="en">
  <head>
    <meta charset="UTF-8" />
    <meta name="viewport" content="width=device-width, initial-scale=1.0" />
    <title>JS Demo</title>
  </head>
  <body>
    <app-main></app-main>
  </body>
</html>
```

This requires you to load and upgrade one component. To do this, you need the start a procedure in `main.js`:

```
import JSX, { GlobalProvider } from '@nyaf/lib';
import { MessageComponent } from './components/message.component';
import { MainComponent } from './components/main.component';

GlobalProvider.bootstrap({
  components: [MainComponent, MessageComponent],
});
```

The two demo components are shown below:

```
import JSX, { GlobalProvider, BaseComponent, CustomElement } from
'@nyaf/lib';

@CustomElement('app-main')
export class MainComponent extends BaseComponent {
  render() {
    return (
      <>
        <h1>Hello NYAF</h1>
        <app-message></app-message>

    );
  }
}
import JSX, { GlobalProvider, BaseComponent, CustomElement } from
'@nyaf/lib';

@CustomElement('app-message')
export class MessageComponent extends BaseComponent {
  render() {
    return <div>Hallo @nyaf</div>;
  }
}
```

As you can see, you use JSX and decorators along with ES2018 import/export instructions.

Improvements

Imagine a main file like this:

```
import JSX, { GlobalProvider } from '@nyaf/lib';

import * as cmp from '@components';

GlobalProvider.bootstrap({
    components: [
        cmp.MainComponent,
        cmp.MessageComponent
    ]
});
```

The import from @components makes it so much more convenient. To set up this local path resolution, you need to create an index file for your components:

```
export * from './main.component';
export * from './message.component';
```

Then, set an alias in webpack.config.js to resolve this file:

```
resolve: {
    extensions: ["*", ".js", ".jsx"],
    alias: {
      "@components": path.join(__dirname, "src/components"),
    },
  }
```

To let Visual Studio Code accept this, too, add this jsconfig.json (look for the key paths):

```
{
  "compilerOptions": {
    "baseUrl": "./src",
    "target": "es6",
    "module": "commonjs",
    "experimentalDecorators": true,
```

```
  "paths": {
    "@components/*": ["./src/components/*"]
  }
},
"include": ["src/**/*"]
}
```

Both, the alias' for WebPack as well as the `paths` key can handle multiple entries for more complex setups.

Bundle Size

For the demo files shown in the code above, the whole bundle is 43.7 KB (11.6 KB zipped). The HTML remains at 230 bytes (squeezed).

With all the loader and polyfill stuff, this is an extremely small footprint for a client app. Forms and Flux Store would add another 10 KBytes roughly.

The @nyaf CLI

The @nyaf CLI currently creates TypeScript projects only. To use Babel and pure JS, refer to the documentation in this section.

Components

Components are the core ingredients. You write components as classes, decorated with the decorator `CustomElement`. This defines a Web Component. The component must be registered, then. This is done by calling the static method `GlobalProvider.bootstrap`.

Registration Support

To support the registration, you use decorators, as mentioned. This makes it quite easy to define a component without knowing the details of the browser's API. The name is determined by `@CustomElement('my-name')`. This is mandatory. The name must follow the common rules of Web Components. This means it must have at least one dash (-) so there is no risk of a collision with common HTML element names.

```
import JSX, { CustomElement } from '@nyaf/lib';

@CustomElement('app-main')
export class MainComponent extends BaseComponent<{}> {

  constructor() {
    super();
  }

  render() {
    return (
      <>
        <h1>Demo</h1>

    );
  }

}
```

Let's go step by step through this simple component.

First, the import includes not only the decorator but the type JSX too. This is necessary if you want to use JSX (or TSX) and let the TypeScript compiler translate the HTML syntax properly. The supporting class comes from @nyaf/lib and has absolutely no relation to React. It has, in some details, a different behavior compared with the JSX used in React. The import is necessary, even if there is no explicit usage in the module. Both the TypeScript transpiler and linter (such as TSLint) know about this and will not complain.

Second, the component has a base class. All @nyaf components are derived from HTMLElement. Currently they don't support inheriting from other element types.

Note also the usage of a base class, which gets a generic that later controls the access to the attributes.

Now, that the component is defined, it must be registered. In a file called main.ts (or wherever your app is bootstrapped) call this:

```
import { GlobalProvider } from '@nyaf/lib';
import { MainComponent } from './components/main.component';

GlobalProvider.bootstrap({
  components: [MainComponent]
});
```

That's it. The component works now. Use it in the HTML part, usually called `.index.html`:

```
<body class="container">
  <app-main></app-main>
</body>
```

Once you have more components, it may look like this:

```
GlobalProvider.bootstrap({
  components: [
    ButtonComponent,
    TabComponent,
    TabsComponent,
    MainComponent
  ]
});
```

The First Component

This section describes how to bring the component to life. I assume that you already have a typical TypeScript setup with `tsconfig.json`, `package.json`, and your favorite packer.

Create a file named `main.ts` in the `src` folder that looks like this:

```
import { GlobalProvider } from '@nyaf/lib';

import { MainComponent } from './main.component';

GlobalProvider.bootstrap({
  components: [MainComponent],
});
```

Create file named main.component.tsx in the same folder (it must be _*.tsx_ if you use JSX). Fill this content in:

```
import JSX, { BaseComponent, CustomElement } from '@nyaf/lib';

@CustomElement('app-main')
export class MainComponent extends BaseComponent {

  constructor() {
    super();
  }

  async render() {
    return await (
      <section>
        <h2>Demo</h2>
          <p>Hello nyaf</p>
      </section>
    );
  }

}
```

Watch the default import for JSX. This *is* required, even if there is no explicit call. The TypeScript transpiler needs this when handling JSX files. It's always JSX, even if you use *.tsx files.

Create a file named index.html in the very same folder and fill it like this:

```
<!DOCTYPE html>
<html lang="en">
<head>
  <meta charset="UTF-8">
  <meta name="viewport" content="width=device-width, initial-scale=1.0">
  <meta http-equiv="X-UA-Compatible" content="ie=edge">
  <title>Hello nyaf</title>
</head>
<body>
```

```
<h1>Hello nyaf</h1>
<app-main></app-main>
<!-- script goes here, either by packer or manually -->
</body>
</html>
```

Your app starts at line 10.

Using the packer configuration you get the index.html file in the ./dist folder, a bundle, and a reference to this bundle to load the script. If you pack manually or keep the scripts separately, add the script tags before the closing <body> element.

Template Features

Template features avoid using creepy JavaScript for interactions and branches. You can use any of the following:

- n-if, n-else

- n-hide, n-show

- n-on-<event> (see the "Events" section)

- n-expand

n-if, n-else

For n-if and n-else, the value will be evaluated and the element using this attribute does or does not render:

```
<div class="main-header"
    n-if={this.props.title !== 't1'}>
  <span>Any content will not render if container doesn't render</span>
</div>
```

If there is an `else` branch, it can direct to a slot template. `<slot>` elements are native Web Component parts.

```
<div class="main-header"
    n-if={this.props.title !== 't1'}
    n-else="noShow">
  <span>Any content will not render if container doesn't render</span>
</div>
<slot name="noShow">
  This is shown instead.
</slot>
```

n-hide, n-show

n-hide and n-show work the same as n-if, but just add an inline style `display: none` (or remove one) if `true` (n-hide) or `false` (n-show).

n-expand

The n-expand attribute expands a group of HTML attributes. Imagine an element like this:

```
<input type="text" placeholder="Name"
       role="search" class="form-input" id="a1 />
```

You may need it several times, each with different id. Instead of repeating the whole set of attributes, an expander can be used to add the static parts:

```
<input n-expand="search" id="a1" />
<input n-expand="search" id="a2" />
<input n-expand="search" id="a3" />
```

To define the expander shown above, you create a class like this:

```
@Expand("search")
export class SearchExpander extends Expander {
  constructor(){
    super();
  }
```

```
'type'="text";
'placeholder'="Name";
'role'="search";
'class'="form-input";
}
```

And yes, those are equal signs in the class. The named 'quoted' properties are only required if the attribute name contains dashes. Finally, add the definition to the global provider:

```
Globalprovider.bootstrap({
  components: [...components], // as usual
  expanders: [SearchExpander]
})
```

That's it—a lot less to write without the effort of creating components. It's just text replacement before the renderer grabs the content, so there's **no** performance impact at runtime. The expander logic does not perform any kebab-pascal conversion as some other tools do (that means the name myProp does not appear as my-prop automatically).

Quick Expanders

Quick expanders are even easier, but more for local expansion:

```
const d = {
  'type': "text";
  'placeholder': "Name";
  'role': "search";
  'class': "materialinput";
}
<app-button  {...d} />
```

It's just pure ECMAScript magic; no code from @nyaf is required.

n-repeat

The basic idea of TSX is to write traditional code using `map` or `forEach` on arrays to create loops. In most cases, this is the best solution. It provides editor support and you can add the full range of JavaScript API features to adjust the result. But sometimes a simple loop is required and the creation of a complete expression creates a lot of boilerplate code. In this case, two variations of loops are provided, both with full editor support, too.

The n-repeat Component

`n-repeat` is a smart component that acts as a helper for common tasks. It's supported by one function for binding:

- `of`: Creates an expression to select a property from a model. The only reason is to have editor support (IntelliSense) without additional tools.

```
<ul>
  <n-repeat source={this.eventData}>
    <li data={of<TBind>(p => p.id)}>{of<TBind>(p => p.name)}</li>
  </n-repeat>
</ul>
```

The n-repeat Attribute

A `@nyaf` template function with the same name exists. This is supported by two other functions for same reason:

- `from`: Defines a data source for repeating; must be an array of objects.

- `select`: Selects a property from the object type the array consists of.

```
<ul>
  <li n-repeat={from<TBind>(this.eventData)}
      data={select<TBind>(p => p.id)} >
      The name is: {select<TBind>(p => p.name)}
  </li>
</ul>
```

Both examples would work with a type definition like this:

```
interface TBind {
  id: number;
  name: string;
}
```

In the component, the data assignment looks like this:

```
// excerpt from a component
private eventData: Array<TBind>;

constructor() {
  super();
  this.eventData = [{ id: 1, name: 'One' }, { id: 2, name: 'Two' },
  { id: 3, name: 'Three' }];
}
```

JSX/TSX

Fundamentally, JSX just provides syntactic sugar for the code line JSX.
createElement(component, props, ...children) function. The transformation and
conversion to JavaScript is made by the TypeScript transpiler. If you use pure JavaScript,
the best tool to compile JSX is Babel.

Be aware that while the main framework with native JSX support is React, @nyaf
has absolutely no relation to React, and the behavior of the code is different.

Introduction

The next examples assume that some code surrounds the snippets or is just the return
value of the render() method.

Here's some TSX code used in a component:

```
<my-button color="blue" shadowSize={2}>
  Click Me
</my-button>
```

This piece of code compiles into the following function call:

```
JSX.createElement(
  'my-button',
  {color: 'blue', shadowSize: 2},
  'Click Me'
)
```

JSX Scope

Since JSX compiles into calls to JSX.createElement, the JSX class must also always be in scope from your TSX code.

For example, both of the imports are necessary in this code, even though React and CustomButton are not directly referenced from JavaScript:

```
import JSX from '@nyaf/lib';

// code omitted for brevity

async render() {
  // return JSX.createElement('custom-button', {color: 'red'}, null);
  return await (<custom-button color="red" />);
}
```

Note that this is a default export, so no curly braces here!

If you don't use a JavaScript bundler and load @nyaf from a <script> tag, it is already in scope as a global object named JSX.

The elements used in the JSX parts are registered globally and there is no additional import required. This is a fundamentally different behavior in comparison to React. In React, the first argument is a type and the elements will render themselves based on the given type. In @nyaf, the first argument is a string, and the constructed element is pushed to the browser as string through innerHTML, and the browser renders the content directly using native code.

Select Elements

Using the HTML 5 API can be boring. Instead of using `querySelector` in the component's code, use a decorator:

```
@Select('#queryId') elementName;
```

The element is filled with the real object (of type `HTMLElement`), then. If the selector pulls several elements, you can enforce a list like this:

```
@Select('a.queryied', true) elementName: QueryList<HTMLAnchorElement>;
```

The second parameter triggers this and the result is `QueryList`, a special type that provides a few useful properties:

```
export interface QueryList<T extends HTMLElement> {
  length: number;
  first: T;
  last: T;
  items: T;
}
```

The generic is just a convenience feature here by TypeScript that helps the editor handle the access to element properties better. At runtime it doesn't exist and the real types are determined by the result of the `querySelectorAll` method call.

Smart Components

Some features do not require additional code. They just need a clever usage of the power of TypeScript and Web Components. To simplify your life, a few of these are predefined as integrated components called Smart Components.

Repeater - n-repeat

The repeater component creates a loop. In the following example, an interface defines a single item. An array with items of this type is provided.

```
import JSX, { CustomElement, BaseComponent, of } from '@nyaf/lib';

interface T {
  id: number;
  name: string;
}

@CustomElement('app-repeater-test')
export class RepeaterTestComponent extends BaseComponent<{}> {
  eventData: any;

  constructor() {
    super();
  }

  clickMe(e) {
    console.log('Button Element Click ', e);
    this.eventData = e;
    super.setup();
  }

  async render() {
    const data: Array<T> = [
      { id: 1, name: 'One' },
      { id: 2, name: 'Two' },
      { id: 3, name: 'Three' }]
    return await (

        <div>
          <ul>
            <n-repeat source={data}>
              <li data={of<T>(p => p.id)}>{of<T>(p => p.name)}</li>
            </n-repeat>
          </ul>
        </div>

    );
  }
}
```

The repeater repeats the array's elements. Each element provides properties you can place anywhere in the body using the of<Type> operator. It is type safe and the editor will help you select the right properties from the given type.

Transparent Outlet n-outlet

This is another outlet that renders into nothing. Normally you would do this:

```
<div n-router-outlet></div>
```

But that would place your component in a div element. If this is disturbing, just use this:

```
<n-outlet></n-outlet>
```

Also, a named variety is available:

```
<n-outlet name="main"></n-outlet>
```

Render Finisher n-finish

Web Components render according to their lifecycle. However, if you have a mix of components and regular HTML elements, the behavior can be weird because the regular elements don't have a lifetime. The best solution is to have a pure tree of Web Components. But if that is not possible and a predictable execution path is necessary, you need to tell the render engine when it's really safe to render the parent element. To do so, add the element <n-finish /> like this:

```
render() {
  return (
    <ul>
      <some-component></some-component>
      <li></li>
      <li></li>
      <li></li>
      <n-finish />
    </ul>
  )
}
```

In this example, the component waits for the lifecycle events of `some-component` but will render everything else immediately. If `some-component` exposes `<li>` tags too, they could appear after the static ones. If the order matters, the `<n-finish>` element helps enforce the execution order.

The Life Cycle

Components have a life cycle. Instead of several events, there is just one method you must override (or ignore if not needed):

```
lifeCycle(cycle: LifeCycle){
  if (cycle === LifeCycle.Load){
    // it's ready to go
  }
}
```

Note that the method has lower case "l." The `LifeCycle`-enum (upper case "L") has these fields:

- `Init`: Start, the constructor is called.

- `Connect`: Component connects to the back end.

- `SetData`: A change in the data object occurred.

- `Load`: The render process is done and the component has been loaded.

- `PreRender`: The render method has been called and content is not yet written to `innerHTML`.

- `Disconnect`: The component is going to be unloaded.

- `Disposed`: After calling the `dispose` method.

The life cycle is also available through an event named `lifecycle`. It's exposed via a property called `onlifecycle` on the element level, too. The events are fired after the internal hook has been called.

State and Properties

There is no explicit difference between state and property. Compared with React, it's much simpler. A state still exists and it supports smart rendering. See Figure A-2.

Make Properties Smart

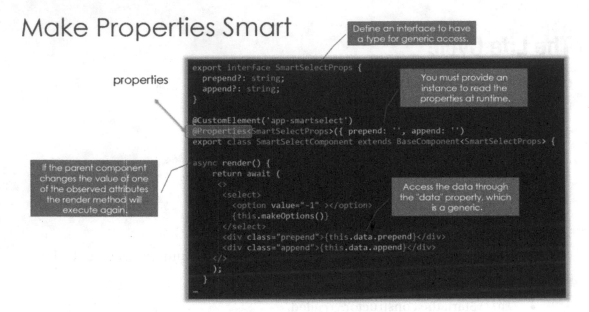

Figure A-2. *Smart properties*

State

To declare a state object, use a generic like this:

```
export class MainComponent extends BaseComponent<{ cnt: number}> {
  // ... omitted for brevity
}
```

The state generic is optional. If there is no state necessary, just use any or an empty object such as { }.

Now two functions are available:

- data: Returns the instance of the data object and contains all properties defined in the generic. This is protected and only available within the class.

- setData: Sets a changed value and, if the value differs, rerenders the component.

A simple counter shows how to use it:

```
export class CounterComponent extends BaseComponent<{ cnt: number }> {

  constructor() {
    super();
    super.setData('cnt',  10);
  }

  clickMeAdd(v: number) {
    super.setData('cnt', super.data.cnt + 1);
  }

  clickMeSub(v: number) {
    super.setData('cnt', super.data.cnt - 1);
  }

  async render() {
    return await (

        <div>
          <button type='button' n-on-click={e => this.clickMeAdd(e)}>
            Add 1
          </button>
          <button type='button' n-on-click={e => this.clickMeSub(e)}>
            Sub 1
          </button>
        </div>
        <pre style='border: 1px solid gray;'>{ this.data.cnt }</pre>

    );
  }
}
```

Properties

Property names in JavaScript are case sensitive and usually written camelcase to improve readability. HTML attribute names are in kebab case (dash-separated) to match HTML standards. By convention, a JavaScript property named `itemName` maps to an HTML attribute named `item-name`. Some libraries exist to execute this conversion and some environments do this implicitly.

Don't start a property name with these characters because they are common prefixes and might already consist of a second part, separated by a dash:

- `on` (for example, `onClick`)

- `aria` (for example, `ariaDescribedby`)

- `data` (for example, `dataProperty`)

Don't use these reserved words for property names. These names are for Web Components only and overwriting can cause malfunctions:

- `slot`

- `part`

- `is`

To use properties, you must define them. Each property is automatically part of the state and once it changes, the component rerenders. See Figure A-3.

```
@CustomElement('app-btn')
@Properties<{ title: string }>({ title: 'Default' })
export class ButtonComponent extends BaseComponent<{ title: string,
cnt: number }> {
  // ... omitted for brevity
}
```

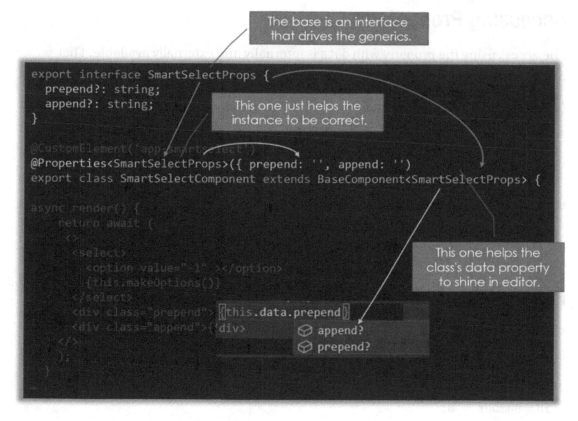

Figure A-3. *Smart property declaration*

The initializer with defaults is **not** optional. You must provide an object that matches the generic.

This is how you use such a component (part of the render method):

```
const someTitle='Demo';
return (<app-btn title={someTitle} />);
```

The @Properties decorator defines all properties that are now monitored (observed) and hence the value is evaluated and rendered. If the value changes, the component renders itself automatically.

Accessing Properties

The access using the property with data is internally and externally available. That means you can retrieve a component and set values like this:

```
(this.querySelector('[data-demo-button]') as any)
   .data
   .text = 'Some demo data';
```

As with setData, internally this will trigger the renderer to rerender the content with the new values, but in this case the trigger is outside the component.

Please note that data is an internal property of the library. To access data- attributes, the HTML 5 API uses the property dataset.

Properties and Models

For a nice-looking view, some decorators applied to class properties control the appearance:

```
export class Model {
  id: number = 0;
  name: string = '';
}

@CustomElement('app-main')
@Properties<{ data: Model }>({ id: 0, name: '' })
export class MainComponent extends BaseComponent {
  // ... omitted for brevity
}
```

Within the component, this model is now present. In the above definition, this.
data contains an actual model. The forms module contains a more sophisticated way to handle a view model with bidirectional data binding. The properties discussed here are for access from a parent component, while the form's module view models handle this internal binding.

Directives

Directives are extensions to host components that are bound to attributes. Think of them as smart handling for data, events, or actions.

Making a Directive

To make a directive, you use the @Directive decorator and the base class BaseDirective. The directive helps register the class. The base class supports the editor and type safety.

A simple example shows how to make any element draggable:

```
@Directive('[directive="drag"]')
export class DragDirective extends BaseDirective {

  constructor(public host: HTMLElement) {
    super(host);
    this.host.draggable = true;
  }

  setup() {
    this.host.addEventListener('dragstart', (e: DragEvent) => {
      e.dataTransfer.setData('text', 'from button');
    });
    this.host.addEventListener('dragover', (e: DragEvent) => {
      e.preventDefault();
    });
  }

}
```

Directives are activated by any kind of selector querySelectorAll process. In this example, I use the [directive="drag"] selector, which is an attribute with a value. To apply this directive, two steps are required:

1. As always, you must register your directive first.

2. You apply the selector to any element (standard HTML, Web Components, or your own stuff; it works everywhere).

197

Registration

The registration is part of the GlobalProvider's bootstrap process:

```
// example import
import { DropTargetDirective, DragDirective } from './directives/index';

GlobalProvider.bootstrap({
  // other parts omitted for brevity
  directives: [DropTargetDirective, DragDirective],
  // other parts omitted for brevity
});
```

Activation

The directive applies once a component renders. This means the directive must be part of a @nyaf Web Component. But the actual assignment can be placed on any HTML element. If you have just one global component and pure HTML in it, then the directive will still work.

To activate the directive, just add the selector to an element:

```
<button type='button' directive='drag'>
Drag me around
</button>
```

The element now becomes a host element for the directive. One directive can be applied to many elements. They are isolated instances. For each occurrence of the selector, a new instance of the directive class is created.

Working with Host Elements

To get access to the host, the directive will modify a property host that is provided by the base class. It's available immediately after the super call of the constructor and injected as a constructor parameter. That's mandatory.

```
constructor(public host: HTMLElement) {
  super(host);
  // here you can safely access the host element
}
```

After the constructor call, the infrastructure calls a method setup. It has no parameters and is not awaitable. It's a good point to add event listeners or add further modifications to the element, as shown in the example above.

The host element is aware of a Shadow DOM, so it might be the host's element object or a shadowed element. This depends on the usage of the @ShadowDOM directive. There is nothing special here, so you can use it directly. The type cast is HTMLElement. This means in TypeScript the properties specific to shadow DOM are not available in the API. In JavaScript, they are still present, though this means you could enforce a cast like this. host as unknown as ShadowRoot. Usually, that's a very rare situation anyway. The idea behind this behavior is to make the Shadow DOM as transparent as possible, without forcing the developer to think about it.

Events

Events are defined by a special instruction. They are attached to document objects, regardless of usage. See Figure A-4.

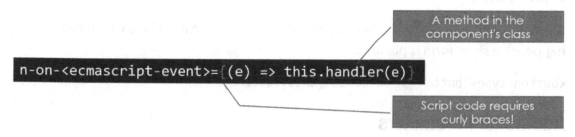

Figure A-4. *Defining an event source*

n-on-event

Events are easy to add directly, using them like n-on-click. All JavaScript events are supported. Just replace click in the example with any other JavaScript event.

```
<button n-on-click={() => this.clickMe()}>OK</button>
```

There is no bind necessary. Events are bound to components anyway.

You can get the (original HTML 5 API) event using a parameter, like e in this example:

```
<button n-on-click={(e) => this.clickMe(e)}>OK</button>
```

Because the method can be bound with or without the event object as a parameter, the method can have an optional parameter like this:

```
clickMe(e?: Event) {

}
```

The Event type conforms to the HTML 5 DOM. Replace the type according to the attached event (MouseEvent, etc.; see https://developer.mozilla.org/en-US/docs/Web/API/Event for details).

Syntax Enhancements

This section shows some variations of the event syntax that might better suit your needs.

Short Form

If you don't need access to the parameters of the event (such as a click, which just happens), a short form is possible:

```
<button type="button" n-on-click={this.clickMe}>
```

Additional Parameters

You can add constant values like this:

```
<button type="button" n-on-click={this.clickMe}>
```

Warning!   Regardless of the type, the received value will be a string type at runtime.

```
<button type="button" n-on-click={(e) => this.clickMe(e, 100)}>
```

This works, but the function will receive "100".

```
<button type="button" n-on-click={(e) => this.clickMe(e, 1 + 2)}>
```

This works, too, but the function will receive "1 + 2". The expression is not being executed! So, this is somehow limited in the current version. You can add multiple parameters, though:

```
<button type="button" n-on-click={(e) => this.clickMe(e, 1, 2)}>
```

```
clickMe(e: Event, a: string, b: string) {
  const r = +a + +b;
}
```

Usually, it doesn't make sense to have calculations on constant values. So in reality this isn't a serious limitation.

Async

You can combine any event with the attribute n-async to make the call to the event's handler function async. This attribute does not take any parameters. The handler method can be decorated with async:

```
<button n-on-click={this.clickMe} n-async>OK</button>
```

```
async clickMe(e?: Event) {
  // handle asynchronously
}
```

Custom Events

Sometimes the JavaScript events are not flexible enough. So you can define your own events. This is done by three simple steps:

- Add a decorator @Events to declare the events (it's an array to declare multiple in one step). This is mandatory.

- Create a CustomEventInit object and dispatch it (this is native Web Component behavior).

- Use the n-on-<myCustomEventName> attribute to attach the event in the parent component.

Imagine a button component like this:

```
@CustomElement('app-button')
@Events(['showAlert'])
export class ButtonComponent extends BaseComponent {
  constructor() {
    super();
  }

  clickMe() {
    const checkEvent: CustomEventInit = {
      bubbles: true,
      cancelable: false,
    };
    super.dispatch('showAlert', checkEvent);
  }

  async render() {
    return await (
      <button type="button" n-on-click={this.clickMe}>
        Demo
      </button>
    );
  }
}
```

The custom event in this example is called showAlert. It's invoked by a click. The element's host component has code like this:

```
<app-button n-on-showAlert={(e) => this.someHandler(e)} />
```

The argument e contains a CustomEvent object. It can carry any number of custom data. The click invoker is just an example. Any action can call a custom event, even a web socket callback, a timer, or an HTTP request result. Both CustomEvent and CustomEventInit have a field named detail that can carry any object or scalar and is the proposed way to transport custom data with the event. The event handler could look like this:

```
<app-button n-on-showAlert={(e) => this.someHandler(e)} />
```

Custom events can be async, too. Just add `n-async` to the element that fires the event and add the `async` modifier to the handler.

Router

Usually we create SPAs. Hence we need a router. The included router is very simple.

First, define an outlet where the components appear:

```
<div n-router-outlet></div>
```

Any kind of parent element will do. The router code sets the property `innerHTML`. Components that are used to provide router content need registration too. They **must** have a name also because that's the way the router internally activates the component.

There is just one default outlet. See Figure A-5 for using named outlets.

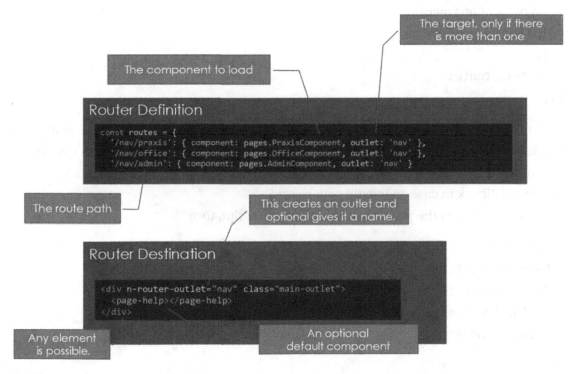

Figure A-5. *The router parts*

Registering Routes

The following code shows how to register routes:

```
let routes = {
  '/': { component: DemoComponent },
  '/about': { component: AboutComponent },
  '/demo': { component: DemoComponent },
  '/contact': { component: ContactComponent },
  '**': { component: DemoComponent }
};

GlobalProvider.bootstrap({
  components: [
    DemoComponent,
    AboutComponent,
    ContactComponent,
    MainComponent
  ],
  routes: routes
});
```

The first entry, '/': { component: DemoComponent }, always exists because it's the default route loaded on start. It's recognized by the '/' key (the position in the array doesn't matter). The entry '**': { component: DemoComponent } is optional and defines a fallback in case an invalid path is used.

You can shorten the property in the bootstrap script, too:

```
const components = [
  DemoComponent,
  AboutComponent,
  ContactComponent,
  MainComponent
];
```

```
GlobalProvider.bootstrap({
  components,
  routes
});
```

Using Routes

To activate a router, you need a hyperlink. The router's code looks for a click onto an anchor tag. An appropriate code snippet to use the routes looks like this:

```
<a href="#/" n-link>Home</a>
<a href="#/about" n-link>About</a>
<a href="#/demo" n-link>Demo</a>
<a href="#/contact" n-link>Contact</a>
<div n-router-outlet></div>
```

The important part here is the n-link attribute. Using this you can distinguish between navigation links for routing and any other anchor tag. You can also use a <button> element or any other. Internally, it's just a click event that's handled and that checks for the attribute then.

Please note the hash sign (#). It's required. No code or strategies here. Write it yourself and then enjoy the very small footprint of the outcome.

Pro Tip! Import the router definition and use additional fields to create a menu directly from router configuration.

If you have some sort of CSS framework running that provides support for menu navigation by classes, just add the class for the currently active element to the n-link attribute like this:

```
<a href="#/" n-link="active">Home</a>
<a href="#/about" n-link="active">About</a>
<a href="#/demo" n-link="active">Demo</a>
<a href="#/contact" n-link="active">Contact</a>
<div n-router-outlet></div>
```

After this, by clicking the hyperlink, the class `active` will be added to the anchor tag. Any click on any `n-link`-decorated tag will remove all of these classes from all of these elements, first. The class' name can differ and you can add multiple classes. It's treated as string internally.

Named Routes

The underlying route definition, the type `Routes`, allows two additional fields (`outlet` and `data`):

```
const routes: Routes = {
  '/': { component: HomeComponent, outlet: 'main' },
  '/docu': {
    component: DocuComponent,
    outlet: 'main',
    data: { notlocal: true}
    },
  '/about': { component: AboutComponent, outlet: 'main' },
  '/demo': { component: DemoComponent, outlet: 'main',
  '/router': { component: RouterComponent, outlet: 'main' },
  '/router/page1': { component: Page1Component, outlet: 'router' },
  '/router/page2': { component: Page2Component, outlet: 'router' },
  '/router/page2/other': { component: Page2Component, outlet: 'other' },
  '/router/page3/other': { component: Page3Component, outlet: 'other' },
  '/contact': { component: ContactComponent }
};
```

With `outlet` you can define a named outlet. If you use it, you must name all routes because there is no fallback currently. The route outlet might reside everywhere. It may look like this:

```
<div n-router-outlet="other"></div>
```

If the route's components deliver `<li>` elements, you can also use something like this to build well-formatted HTML:

```
<ul n-router-outlet="other"></div>
```

There is no difference on the link side. The decision to address another outlet is made in the configuration only. If the outlet doesn't exist, nothing happens and a warning appears on the console (in DEBUG mode).

In the example, I use routes that look like child routes. That's a hint for the intended behavior, but it's technically not necessary to do so. The resolver is very simple and doesn't care about routes. It just matches the string and seeks the outlet.

Additional Data

The last example showed another field named data. This is a dictionary with arbitrary data just stored here. If you set up navigation dynamically based on the configuration data, you can control the behavior in a well-defined way. However, there is no code intercepting these data. It's the task of the implementer to do something useful here.

Special Values

If you use data: { title: 'Some Title' }, the value in the field title is being written into the website's title field. This way it appears on the tab (or header bar in Electron). If it's omitted, it's not set at all.

Navigating to Route

You can navigate by code:

```
GlobalProvider.navigateRoute('/my-route');
```

The outlet is pulled from the configuration, but if provided as a second parameter it can be overwritten.

Hint   In the link elements you use the '#' prefix. In the navigateRoute method this is not necessary and hence not allowed.

Route Events

The router fires two events available through the static `GlobalProvider` class like this:

```
GlobalProvider.routerAction.addEventListener('navigate', (evt) => {
  const route = evt.detail;
  evt.cancel = true;    // optionally cancel before execution
}

GlobalProvider.routerAction.addEventListener('navigated', (evt) => {
  const route = evt.detail;
  // this event can't be cancelled
}
```

If you have a dynamic component and you set the event handler, don't forget to remove the event handler in the dispose callback.

Shadow DOM

By default the Shadow DOM is **not** used. If it was used, it would mean that styles were isolated. No global styles would be available, then.

One option to activate the Shadow DOM is using this decorator:

```
@ShadowDOM()
```

A parameter can be set explicitly. This is some kind of coding style, a more expressive form:

```
@ShadowDOM(true | false)
```

Another interesting option controls the style behavior:

```
@UseParentStyles()
```

- The decorator `ShadowDOM` must be set; otherwise the decorator @ `UseParentStyle` does nothing.

- If active, it copies all global styles into component so they work as expected even in a Shadow DOM.

> It's a tradeoff. The Shadow DOM increases performance and brings isolation. Copying many styles decreases performance and contradicts isolation.

See this example for a common usage scenario:

```
@CustomElement('app-contact')
@ShadowDOM()
@UseParentStyles()
export class ContactComponent extends BaseComponent {
  // omitted for brevity
}
```

The Shadow DOM goes well along with the usage of slots. A typical example is a tabs component, which is shown next. Tabs are a form of navigation for websites, similar to the browser's tabs.

Example with Shadow DOM

It starts with the definition of a single tab.

Single Tab

The following code defines a single tab component:

```
import JSX, {
  BaseComponent,
  CustomElement,
  ShadowDOM,
  UseParentStyles,
  LifeCycle } from '@nyaf/lib';

@CustomElement('app-slot-tab')
@ShadowDOM(    )
export class SlotTabComponent extends BaseComponent<{}> {

  private _title: string;
```

```
constructor() {
  super();
  this.classList.add('hide');
}

async render() {
  return await (
    <div id={this.getAttribute('data-id')}>
      <slot></slot>
    </div>
  );
}

public get title() {
  return this._title;
}

public set title(value) {
  this._title = value;
}

}
```

The <slot> element is the content target. The id is used to address the tab (to open it, actually).

Tabs Container

Second, look at the container that handles multiple tabs:

```
import JSX, {
  BaseComponent,
  CustomElement,
  LifeCycle,
  Events,
  ShadowDOM,
  UseParentStyles,
  uuidv4 } from '@nyaf/lib';
```

```
interface TabStore {
  node: Node;
  targetId: string;
  id: string;
}

interface IMaterialTabsDefaultConfig {
  materialtabsDeferred?: number;
  deep?: boolean;
  fixedTabs?: boolean;

  clsComponent?: string;
  clsTab?: string;
  clsTabActive?: string;
  clsMarker?: string;

  onBeforeTabOpen?();
  onTabOpen?();
  onTabsScroll?();
  onTabsCreate?();
};

// tslint:disable-next-line:max-classes-per-file
@CustomElement('app-slot-tabs')
@Events(['all'])
@ShadowDOM(true)
@UseParentStyles(true)
export class SlotTabsComponent extends BaseComponent<{}> {

  private tabChildren: TabStore = ;

  constructor() {
    super();
  }
```

```
async render() {
  let first = 0;
  const tabHeaders = Array.prototype
              .slice
              .call(this.children)
              .map((child: Element) => {
    const targetId: string = child.id ?? '_' + uuidv4();
    child.setAttribute('id', targetId);
    this.tabChildren.push({
      node: child,
      targetId,
      id: child.id
    });
    return (
      <li class='nav-item'>
        <a class={'nav-link ' + (0 === first++ ? 'active' : '')}
           href={`#${targetId}`} >
          {child.getAttribute('title')}
        </a>
      </li>
    );
  });
  return await (

      <ul role="nav" class="nav nav-tabs">
        {tabHeaders}
      </ul>
      <div class='row'>
        <div class='col'>
          <slot></slot>
        </div>
      </div>

  )
}
```

```
lifeCycle(lc: LifeCycle) {
  if (lc === LifeCycle.Load) {
    let first = 0;
    this.shadowRoot.querySelectorAll('li')
      .forEach(li => {
        li.addEventListener('click',
              (e: Event) => this.selectTab(e));
        if (first === 0) {
          this.openTab(li.querySelector('a').getAttribute('href'));
        }
        first++;
      });
  }
}

private selectTab(e: Event) {
  let targetId = (e.target as HTMLElement).getAttribute('href');
  if (!targetId) {
    const innerA = (e.target as HTMLElement).querySelector('a');
    if (innerA) {
      targetId = innerA.getAttribute('href');
    }
  }
  this.openTab(targetId);
  e.preventDefault();
  e.cancelBubble = true;
  return false;
}

async setTab(id: string): Promise<void> {
  const targetId = this.tabChildren
      .filter((child) => child.id === id)
      .shift()
      .targetId;
```

```
    // use shadowRoot because it is shadowed
    this.openTab(`#${targetId}`);
    return Promise.resolve();
  }

  // the visible tabs are in the shadow-root,
  // the content is outside in the document
  private openTab(targetId: string) {
    const tabs = this.shadowRoot.querySelectorAll('li > a');
    // const tab = this.querySelector<HTMLElement>(targetId);
    const a = this.shadowRoot.querySelector(`[href="${targetId}"]`);
    // hide all
    const tabContent = this.querySelectorAll('app-slot-tab');
    tabContent.forEach((t: HTMLElement) => {
      t.classList.add('d-none');
    });
    // deactivate all
    tabs.forEach(t => {
      t.classList.remove('active');
    });
    // activate
    a.classList.add('active');
    // move the marker
    // make tabContent visible
    const currentTab = this.querySelector('app-slot-tab' + targetId);
    currentTab.classList.remove('d-none');
  }

}
```

It's the complete handling of tabs and the relevant styles. The CSS classes used in the example are pulled from Bootstrap 4.

Usage of the Tabs

The usage is quite simple. Just add as many tabs as required:

```
<app-slot-tabs id='demoTabs'>
  <app-slot-tab title='Store Counter' id='d1'>
    <app-store-counter id='s1' cnt={42}></app-store-counter>
  </app-slot-tab>
  <app-slot-tab title='Store Data' id='d2'>
    <app-store-data id='s2'></app-store-data>
  </app-slot-tab>
</app-slot-tabs>
```

Shadow DOM and Styles

The Shadow DOM provides full isolation. The @UseParentStyles decorator contradicts this. A better way is to include styles "per component." Have a look at an example first:

```
@CustomElement('app-directive')
@ShadowDOM()
export class DirectiveComponent extends BaseComponent<any> {

  async render() {
    return await (

        <button type='button' directive='drag' part='drag-button'>
          Drag me around
        </button>
        <div directive='drop' part='drop-zone'>

        </div>

    );
  }

}
```

The important part here is, despite the @ShadowDOM decorator, the part attribute. It makes the shadowed component accessible (penetrable) for special external styles using the ::part pseudo-selector. A stylesheet could look like this:

```
app-directive::part(drop-zone) {
  border: 1px solid silver;
  width: 100px;
  height: 100px;
}
app-directive::part(drag-button) {
  background-color: green;
  padding: 5px;
}
```

This style is provided globally, not as part of the component, but it applies to this component only and only in shadow mode.

Note that using the regular CSS syntax, such as app-directive[part="drop-zone"] would not work because it can't penetrate the Shadow DOM.

This is not a feature of @nyaf; it's default Web Component behavior. You may face some issues with older browser versions that don't understand the ::part selector properly. Consider adding a polyfill if needed.

Services

Once in a while we need to get access to an injectable service. That's also a task for a decorator to extract that kind of infrastructure code from the component's body.

```
@CustomElement('app-main')
@InjectService('localNameA', ServiceClass1)
@InjectService('localNameB', ServiceClass2.instance, true)
export class MainComponent extends BaseComponent<{}> {
```

```
// ... omitted for brevity

async render() {
  let data = await this.services('localNameA').
  callAnyServiceFunctionHereAsync();
}

}
```

this.services is a function that returns an instance of the service. Services are a singleton on the level of the local name. The same name used in different components will return the same instance. Using a different name will create a new instance.

Async is an option. It can by sync, too. However, the render process is always asynchronous internally.

The third option of @InjectService allows us to define a singleton. Instead of providing a type for the second parameter of the decorator, here you must provide an instance. The same name will be shared across components.

Forms Module

Forms provide these basic features:

- UI control decorators (example: @Hidden() to suppress a property in a dynamic table)

- Validation decorators (example: @MinLength(50) or @Required() to manage form validation)

- Data binding using a model declaration decorator called @ViewModel and a bind attribute named n-bind

Form validation is a key part of any project. However, CSS frameworks require different strategies to handle errors and so on. Hence, the @nyaf/forms library provides a simple way (just like a skeleton) to give you the direction, but the actual validation implementation logic is up to you to build.

It's the same for the UI decorators. It's a convenient way to add hidden properties to view models. There is no logic to read these values; it is up to you to implement this. However, the decorators make your life a lot easier.

The binding logic is almost complete, and once you have a decorated model, it syncs the UI automagically.

How It Works

For full support, you need view models, the registration on top of the component, and access to the model binder.

1.   View models are plain TypeScript classes with public properties enhanced by decorators.

2.   The registration with the decorator @ViewModel() on top of the component's class.

3.   The modelbinder comes through implementing the interface IModel<ViewModelType>.

View Models in Components

For a nice-looking view, some decorators applied to class properties control the appearance. Use the decorator @ViewModel<T>(T) to define the model. The generic is the type; the constructor parameter defines the default values (it's **mandatory**). To get access to the model binder, just implement the interface IModel as show below:

```
export class Model {
  @Hidden()
  id: number = 0;

  @Required()
  name: string = '';
}
```

```
@CustomElement('app-main')
@ViewModel<Model>(Model)
export class MainComponent
        extends BaseComponent<{}>
        implements IModel<Model> {
  // ... omitted for brevity
}
```

Within the component, the model binder is present through the property `this.model`. It's the only property and it's added automatically by the decorator. The interface just helps the TypeScript transpiler to understand that the property exists.

```
this.model. ...// do something with it
```

An actual object is already assigned to the property by a so-called model binder. At any time in the constructor, in load life cycle, or later with a user action, you can add a new model if you need. That's a rare condition, though. Use this code:

```
this.model.scope = new Model();
```

However, the `@ViewModel` decorator does exactly this for you, so in case of a new blank instance there is no need to assign a new object to the `scope` property.

It's not necessary to keep a reference to the instance; the model binder does this internally for you. The derived class is a `Proxy`. If you now bind the properties using n-bind as described below, the model will be in sync with the user interface. If you want to programmatically access the current state, just retrieve the model:

```
let userName: string = this.model.scope.userName;
```

If you wish to access the `Proxy` at any time in code or not using the binding in templates, this would be sufficient:

```
private modelProxy: Model;

constructor() {
  super();
  this.modelProxy = this.model.scope;
}
```

The setter of scope takes an instance, wraps it into a Proxy, assigns the binders, and the getter returns the Proxy. Changes to the model will now reflect in bound HTML elements immediately:

```
let userName: string = 'Test';
this.model.scope.userName = userName; // immediately invoke binders
```

View Models

First, you need view models. Then, you decorate the properties with validation and hint decorators.

Why Use View Models?

View models form an abstraction layer between code and pure user interface. They appear in many architectural patterns, such as Model-View-Control (MVC), Model-View-ViewModel (MVVM), and similar constructs. A component library such as @nyaf is a different kind of pattern, but the basic need for a model is still valid.

The view model is essential when you want a separation of concerns between your domain model (data model) and the rest of your code.

Decoupling and separation of concerns are two of the most crucial parts of modern software architectures. Models can contain code, have actions, and work as a distinct translator between the domain model and the view. It's not the same as the business logic. It's a layer between such a layer and the user interface (UI). A UI contains logic to control visible elements, such as tooltips, hints, and validation information. All this has no or only a weak relation to the underlying business logic. Mixing the both will create code that is hard to maintain, complex, and difficult to read. In software technology, we often talk about so-called software entropy. This is the process of code changing over time into an even harder-to-manage form, with a lot of hacks, bells, and whistles nobody understands completely and that will eventually start to fail. Levels of abstraction help to delay this process (it's an illusion that you can avoid it entirely). View models are hence an essential part of a good architecture.

The Flux architecture, delivered by the @nyaf/store module, seems to address a similar approach using store models and binding. However, this part is entirely devoted to business logic. It's exactly that kind of abstraction we need to make great software not only by great design and an amazing stack of features, but by sheer quality, stability, with maintainable code, hard to break, and almost free of nasty bugs.

Creating a View Model

A view model could look like this:

```
export class UserViewModel {

  @Hidden()
  id: Number = 0;

  @Display('E-Mail', 'E-Mail address')
  @Required()
  @MaxLength(100)
  @Email()
  email: string = '';

  @Display('Phone Number', 'The user\'s phone')
  @Required('Please, the phone number is required')
  @MaxLength(20)
  phoneNumber: string = '';

  @Display('User Name', 'The full name')
  @Required()
  @MaxLength(100)
  userName: string = '';

}
```

The last (optional) parameter of the validation decorators is a custom error message.

Validation Decorators

Validation decorators can be used together with the binding. After a binding action takes place, usually after a change by the user, the state of the bound model updates and can be retrieved immediately. Elements bound to validation signals can use the state to show/hide elements or control sending data in code. The property names are the same as the respective decorators, just all lowercase. See Table A-1.

Table A-1. *Decorators*

Decorator	Usage
@MaxLength	The maximum length of a text input
@MinLength	The minimum length of a text input
@Pattern	A regular expression that is used to test the text or number input
@Range	A range (from-to) for either numerical values or dates
@Required	Makes the field mandatory
@EMail	Checks input against a (very good) regular expression to test for a valid email pattern
@Compare	A comparison with another field, usually for password comparison
@Custom	Provides a static validation function as a callback for any custom validation

UI Decorators (Property Level)

UI decorators control the appearance of elements. Not all have an immediate effect, but it's very helpful while creating components to have metadata available. See Table A-2.

Table A-2. *UI Decorators*

Decorator	Usage
@Display	Determines the label's name and an (optional) tooltip
@DisplayGroup	Groups components in `<fieldset>` elements. Can be ordered inside the form.
@Hidden	Makes a hidden field
@Sortable	Makes a column sortable in table views
@Filterable	Adds a filter in table views
@Placeholder	A watermark that appears in empty form fields
@ReadOnly	Forces a particular render type
@TemplateHint	What kind of field (text, number, date, …) and additional styles or classes

The UI decorators do not enforce any specific behavior. In fact, they do almost nothing in an application without explicit support. The decorators create hidden properties you can retrieve when building the UI. This way you can control the behavior of the app by setting the decorators. It's some sort of abstraction between the view model and the UI.

Mapping the Properties

The actual properties are of the form __propName__fieldName, which means you must add the decorated property name at the end to retrieve the property specific value. As an example, the displayText property, created by the decorator @Display, and placed on a property email, can be retrieved by this code:

```
const text = this.model['__displayText__email'];
```

However, the internal names may change and to avoid any issues a mapping with external names is available. Table A-3 shows the properties the decorators create.

Table A-3. *Decorator Properties*

Decorator function	Properties
Display	text, order, desc
DisplayGroup	grouped, name, order, desc
Hidden	is
Sortable	is
Filterable	is
Placeholder	has, text
ReadOnly	is
TemplateHint	has, params, name

Special Decorators

There is one more decorator that doesn't just define the UI behavior but has some internal behavior. See Table A-4.

Table A-4. *The @Translate Decorator*

Decorator	Usage
@Translate	For i18n of components

This decorator can be placed on top of the view model, on class level, or on a specific property:

```
export class ContactModel {

  constructor(init?: ContactModel) {
    if (init) {
      this.name = init.name;
      this.email = init.email;
    }
  }
}
```

```
@Translate(json)
@Display('Contact Name')
@Required()
name = '';
}
```

The function expects a JSON file with translation instructions. The translation converts the text on the properties to another language (here in German as an example):

```
const json = {
  'Contact Name': 'Kontaktname'
};
```

This decorator is experimental and will change in the near future to reflect a more powerful approach.

Providing the View Model

To make a view model accessible, you use the @ViewModel(T) decorator. More about this in the section on data binding later in the appendix.

Data Binding

Data binding is one of the most important features in component development. It brings an immediate effect in simplifying the data presentation layer. Instead of the chain "select" ➤ "set" ➤ "listen" ➤ "change," you simply bind an object's properties to an element's attributes. This can go in both directions.

Template Language Enhancements

@nyaf has a simple template language extension for binding. For forms, it's just one more command for any input element, n-bind. Consider this excerpt from a component:

```
model: ModelBinder<UserViewModel>; // instance created by decorator

async render() {
  const model: UserViewModel = new UserViewModel(); // or where ever the
  model comes from
```

```
return await (

    <form>
      <input n-bind="Name: value      " />
    </form>
  );
}
```

Now the field knows everything about how to render and how to validate. The first item ("value") is the HTML element's property you bind to. The second is the model's property name ("Name").

For a good UI you need a label, usually:

```
<label n-bind="userName: innerText     " />
```

Terms and Parts

To understand the binding, you must know what a view model is and what role the model plays inside the form.

View Model

The actual definition of the model that is bindable is provided through the decorator @ViewModel(T). T is a type (class) that has properties decorated with validation and UI decorators. More about this can be found in the section on view models above.

IModel Interface

The @ViewModel decorator creates an instance of the model class. The interface enforces the visibility of the model in the component. The definition is quite easy:

```
export interface IModel<VM extends object> {
    model: ModelBinder<VM>;
}
```

The instance of the ModelBinder gives access to all binding features.

Binding Handlers

Binding handlers are small function calls that handle the data flow between the view model property and element attribute. There are a few default binding handlers available.

Smart Binders

Instead of using the string form you can use the TSX syntax and binding functions:

- to: Generic function to bind a property to the default attribute using a custom binder optionally

- bind: Generic function to bind a property to any attribute

- val: Bind validation decorators to an attribute. See validation.

See the other "Smart Binders" section for details.

Creating Forms

The model is provided by the @ViewModel decorator and the IModel<T> interface like this:

```
@ViewModel(ModelType)
export class component extends BaseComponent<any> implements
IModel<ModelType> {

  async render() {
    return await (
      <form>
        <label n-bind="userName: innerText    " for="un"/>
        <input n-bind="userName: value     " id="un" />
        <br />
        <label n-bind="city: innerText    " for="city"/>
        <input n-bind="city: value     " id ="city" />
      </form>
    )
  }

}
```

The form now binds the data. It's bidirectional or unidirectional depending on the chosen binding handler.

Standard Binding Handlers

The forms module comes with a couple of predefined binding handlers, shown in Table A-5.

Table A-5. *Binding Handlers*

Name	Key	Direction	Applies to	Base Element
Default…	'default'	uni	Attribute	HTMLElement
Checked…	'checked'	bi	attribute checked	HTMLInputElement
Text…	'innerText'	uni	property textContent	HTMLElement
Value…	'value'	bi	attribute value	HTMLInputElement
Visibility…	'visibility'	uni	style visibility	HTMLElement
Display…	'display'	uni	style display	HTMLElement

The actual handler names are ***BindingHandler (Default... is actually DefaultBindingHandler). If in the binding attribute the text form is used ('innerText: userName'), the key value determines the used handler. The handler provides the active code that handles the change call and applies the changed value to the right target property. That can be any property the element type supports, directly or indirectly, anywhere in the object structure. Such a deeper call happens in the style handlers, especially VisibilityBindingHandler and DisplayBindingHandler.

Smart Binders

There is an alternative syntax that provides full type support:

```
<label
  n-bind={to<ContactModel>(c => c.email, 'innerText', Display)}>
</label>
```

The function to<Type> from the @nyaf/forms module has these syntax variations:

```
to<ViewModel>(propertyExpression, handlerKey)
to<ViewModel>(propertyExpression, null, BindingHandlerType)
to<ViewModel, ElementType>(propertyExpression, handlerKey)
to<ViewModel, ElementType>(propertyExpression, null, BindingHandlerType)
to<ViewModel>(propertyExpression, handlerKey, UIDecoratorType)
to<ViewModel>(propertyExpression, null, BindingHandlerType,
UIDecoratorType)
to<ViewModel, ElementType>(propertyExpression, handlerKey, UIDecoratorType)
to<ViewModel, ElementType>(propertyExpression, null, BindingHandlerType,
UIDecoratorType)
```

The generic parameters are as follows:

1. The view model type. This is mandatory.

2. The element type. This is optional, if omitted it falls back to HTMLElement.

The parameters are as follows:

1. A lambda expression to select a property type safe (c => c.name). This is mandatory.

2. The key of a UI attribute. Any property available in HTMLElement is allowed (and it's restricted to them). If a binder is provided, it's used and determines the attribute, hence the value can be null.

3. The (optional) type of decorator that's used to pull data from. If it's omitted, the actual data appear.

Obviously you could think about writing this:

```
<input
  n-bind={to<ContactModel>(c => c.email, 'value')} />
```

This will be rejected by the compiler because the property value doesn't exist in HTMLElement. To provide another type, just use a second generic type parameter:

```
<input
  n-bind={to<ContactModel, HTMLInputElement>(c => c.email, 'value')} />
```

Here you tell the compiler that it's safe to use HTMLInputElement and so the editor allows value as the second parameter. An even smarter way is to use the lambda here, too:

```
<input
  n-bind={to<ContactModel, HTMLInputElement>(c => c.email, c => c.value)}
/>
```

But both ways are type safe, even the string is following a constrain. The string is usually shorter; the lambda might use an earlier suggestion from IntelliSense.

The binding behavior is tricky but powerful. The intention is to provide rock-solid type safety. You must provide an element attribute that really exists to make a successful binding. Everything else wouldn't make any sense. But to actually bind properly, you must provide a binding handler that can handle this particular binding.

Multi-Attribute Binding

The n-bind attribute is exclusive, so you can bind only one attribute. That's fine for most cases, but sometimes you need multiple bindings. In Angular, this is easy through the binding syntax around any element (<input [type]="source" [value]="model">). However, this requires a template compiler and additional editor support. To overcome the limitations here, the bind function is available.

In this example, two properties are bound:

```
<input
  value={bind<T>(c => c.email)}
  type={bind<T>(c => c.toggleType)}
  n-bind />
```

The n-bind is still required to efficiently trigger the binder logic. It's now empty, though (default value is true internally). Please note that you can't bind to deeper structures in the current version (e.g. style.border={bind<T>()} is not possible.) This is typically a way to bind styles in Angular, but this would violate the rule that standard @nyaf templates shall be standard TSX files that any editor can handle without additional tool support. To support a scenario with style binding, refer to "Custom Binders" section.

If the binding handler is not provided, it falls back to a `DefaultBindingHandler`, which binds unidirectional to the assigned attribute. This has two limitations. First, it's always unidirectional. Second, it can bind only to attributes of `HTMLElement`. Object properties, such as `textContent` or `innerText,` cannot be reached this way. This is indeed the same with Angular, where you need to encapsulate elements in custom components to reach hidden properties, but in @nyaf there is a much smarter way.

Imagine you'll bind to whatever, just by assigning another binding handler:

```
<input value={bind<T>(c => c.email, ValueBindingHandler)} n-bind />
```

The binding handler may write into whatever property you like, even those not available as attributes. See the "Custom Binders" section for more details.

Even More Smartness

You may also define your component as a generic. This avoids repeating the model name over and over again. Imagine this:

```
// ContactModel defined elsewhere
export class ContactComponent<T extends ContactModel>
        extends BaseComponent<any>
        implements IModel<ContactModel> {
```

And in this case, you can use a shorter form to express the binding:

```
<label n-bind={to<T>(c => c.email, c => c.innerText)} />
```

T is a placeholder here. Use any name you like to define a "type."

That's cool, isn't it? Now you have a fully type-safe binding definition in the middle of the TSX part without any additions to regular HTML.

And in case you have special properties beyond HTMLElement, than just provide the proper type like you did before:

```
<input n-bind={to<T, HTMLInputElement>(c => c.email, c => c.value)} />
```

This gives full type support in any editor for all types; even custom Web Components will work here.

This technique avoids parsing the template, and the missing parser makes the package so small. The function simply returns a magic string that the model binder class recognizes at runtime. The function call with a generic helps the editor to understand the types and avoids mistakes.

Validation

Form validation is painful to program from scratch. @nyaf/forms provides an integrated but flexible validation system.

View Model Decorators

First, you need a view model that has validation decorators. It's the same kind of model used for regular binding. Again, here is an example:

```
export class UserViewModel {
  @Hidden()
  id: Number = 0;

  @Display('E-Mail', 'E-Mail address')
  @Required()
  @MaxLength(100)
  @Email()
  email: string = '';

  @Display('Phone Number', "The user's phone")
  @Required('Please, the phone number is required')
  @MaxLength(20)
  phoneNumber: string = '';
```

```
@Display('User Name', 'The full name')
@Required()
@MaxLength(100)
userName: string = '';
}
```

Especially the validation decorators are in control of the validation (`Required`, `MaxLength`, and so on). In the binding instruction, you tell the environment with what decorator a property has to be connected.

State

The validation state is available through `state`:

```
this.model.state = {
  isValid: boolean,
      errors: { [key: string]: string },
  validators    :{ [key: string]: ErrorState },
  summary: { [key: string]: { [validator: string]: string }}
}
```

It's supervised. After the component is rendered, the property `this.model.state` holds the state of the model.

After a binding happens, the validators are executed and the instance values change. You can retrieve the values in a method or an event handler. To set UI elements interactively, immediately, you again use the `n-bind` attribute and the appropriate binding function like `to` and `bind`.

Binding to Validators

An error message is just regular output (the class values are taken from Bootstrap and they're not needed by the **@nyaf/forms** module):

```
<form>
  <label n-bind="innerText: userName" for="un"/>
  <input n-bind="value: userName" id="un">
```

```
<div class="text text-danger"
     n-bind={val<ViewModel>(e => e.userName,
                            Required,
                            DisplayBindingHandler)}>
</div>
</form>
```

Validators can provide the error text, too. This is driven by decorators. The decorators fall back to a simple plain English error message if you don't provide anything. You can, however, provide any kind of message in the decorator. If you need i18n messages, just add the @Translate decorator as a parameter decorator to the message parameter.

Distinguish between different validators like this:

```
<form>
  <label n-bind="innerText: userName" for="un"/>
  <input n-bind="value: userName" id="un">
  <span class="text text-danger"
        n-bind={val<ViewModel>(e => e.userName,
                               MaxLength,
                               DisplayBindingHandler)}>
  </span>
</form>
```

The smart binder val is the key ingredient here. It takes three parameters:

1. An expression to access the model's actual value

2. A validator for which the binding is responsible (must also be on the view model's property)

3. A display handler that pulls the values and assigns them to the right property

In the above example, the view model has this property:

```
@Required()
@MaxLength(100)
userName: string = '';
```

Now, the binding instruction looks like this:

```
val<ViewModel>(e => e.userName, MaxLength, DisplayBindingHandler)
```

The DisplayBindingHandler is smart enough to know that it's bound to an error message. It now reads the second parameter that is MaxLength. It binds these two parts.

First, it binds the error message to textContent. That's a static assignment. Second, it binds the display style to the isValid method of the view model. This method is set through the MaxLength decorator and knows how to determine the state 'maxlength'. The property is bound through the scope's proxy dynamically and once the value changes, irrespective of the source of the change, it fires an event and the model binder holds a subscriber for this. Here, the value is taken and handed over to the isValid method. This method is bound to the handler, which sets the style accordingly. That setting is reversed, meaning that the value true makes the message invisible, while the value false makes the message visible (isValid === false tells you an error occurred).

If you use the DisplayBindingHandler or VisibilityBindingHandler directly, without validation but in conjunction with binding operations, then they will work straight: true makes an element visible and false invisible.

Handler Behavior

The DisplayBindingHandler sets display: none or display: block. The VisibilityBindingHandler sets visibility: hidden or visibility: visible. They are the most basic handlers and are available out of the box.

If you need other values, you must write a new handler with the desired behavior. This is, fortunately, extremely simple. Here is the source code for the handlers:

```
export class DisplayBindingHandler implements IBindingHandler {
  react(binding: Binding): void {
    binding.el.style.display = binding.value ? 'block' : 'none';
  }
}

export class VisibilityBindingHandler implements IBindingHandler {
  react(binding: Binding): void {
    binding.el.style.visibility = binding.value ? 'visible' : 'hidden';
  }
}
```

The `Binding` instance, provided internally, delivers a Boolean value. The element `el` is the element that has the `n-bind={val<T>()}` instruction. `T` is the model that drives the content using decorators.

Additional Information

Objects are always set (not undefined), so you don't have to test first. The property names are same as the decorators, but in lowercase:

- @MaxLength: `maxlength`
- @MinLength: `minlength`
- @Pattern: `pattern`
- @Range: `range`
- @Required: `required`
- @EMail: `email`
- @Compare: `compare`

Custom Binders

Custom binders help binding to specific properties. They can be used like the embedded binders, which act just as examples and are used the same way.

Implementing a Custom Binder

A custom binder handles the binding procedure when binding a view model property to an element attribute. It consists of three parts:

1. The binding setup (`bind`)

2. The binder into the element (a property change leads to an attribute change)

3. The listener (an attribute change event leads to an updated model property)

Step 2 and 3 are both optional. Omitting them leads to a unidirectional binding in one or another direction:

```
@BindName('VisibilityBinder')
export class VisibilityBinder<T extends ConfirmSuccessErrorComponent>
        implements IBindingHandler
{
  bind(binding: Binding): void {
    (binding.el as T).addEventListener('done', (e) => {
      this.listener(binding, e);
    })
    this.react(binding);
  }
  react(binding: Binding): void {
    (binding.el as T).visibility = !!binding.value;
  }
  listener(binding: Binding): void {
    const value = (binding.el as T).visibility;
    binding.value = value;
  }
}
```

Note here that, despite the base class, the decorator @BindName is required. The argument is the name of the class. In the views code, the binder class name can be used to determine the behavior. But if the project is packed by an aggressive packer, the names of the classes might be minified. The code compares the names and due to different minification steps it could happen that the comparison fails. The decorator writes the name into an internal property and the compare code can retrieve this properly. If the view code uses strings instead of types, using this decorator is not necessary.

How It Works

First, you need to implement IBindingHandler:

```
export interface IBindingHandler {
  bind?(binding: Binding | ValidatorBinding): void;
  react(binding: Binding | ValidatorBinding, property?: string): void;
  listener?(binding: Binding | ValidatorBinding, e?: Event): void;
}
```

A handler must react to something, but everything else is optional. See this line:

```
export class VisibilityHandler<T extends ConfirmComponent>
      implements IBindingHandler
```

The generic is optional. It allows the definition of the target element. If it's omitted, it falls back to HTMLElement. You can use any HTML 5 element type or any custom Web Component type (as in the example).

The bind method is called implicitly by the infrastructure. If it doesn't exist, it's ignored. The only reason to use it is to attach an event listener. You may also consider calling react immediately to sync the data, but it depends on the actual behavior of the element and may result in an additional binding process while loading the form.

The method react is called from the view model proxy instance each time the value changes. Write code here to assign the data to any property of the target element.

The method listener is optional and is called once the target element raises an event. You can access the original event if provided.

A Simple Binder

How simple a binder can be is shown here with the already embedded unidirectional default binder:

```
@BindName('DefaultBindingHandler')
export class DefaultBindingHandler implements IBindingHandler {
  react(binding: Binding, property: string): void {
    binding.el[property] = binding.value;
  }
}
```

The only difference here is that the ModelBinder class intercepts the access and delivers the name of the attribute as a second parameter. This is a special behavior and the default handler can handle this.

Note that all examples have almost no error and exception handling. Add them if you want a more robust application.

Installation of Forms Module

Install the package:

```
npm i @nyaf/forms -S
```

The type definitions required for TypeScript are part of the packages and no additional type libraries are required.

Dependencies

This package depends on @nyaf/lib only.

The Flux Store

This module is the store implementation, a simple Flux variant without the burden of Redux. It strictly follows the Flux pattern and brings, once fully understood, a great amount of strict programming style to your application. It brings state to your SPA. Outside of a SPA it's not useful. See Figure A-6.

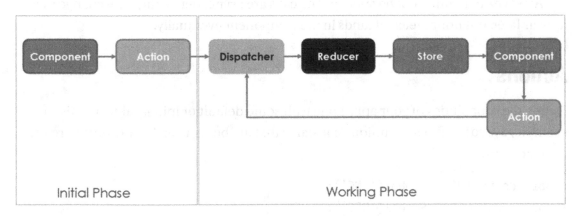

Figure A-6. *The Flux model*

How It Works

It's very much like Redux, but it makes use of decorators to write less code. It's a good strategy to create one global store in your app. Leave it empty if there are no global actions, but make it global if you have such actions.

Then, define three parts for each implementation:

- **Actions** that the component offers (such as SEARCH, LOAD, SET, REMOVE, you name it)

- **Reducers** that are pure function calls that do what your business logic requires (change data, call services)

- A **State** object that holds all the data. The reducer can change the state, but nobody else can.

In the component, you have two tasks:

1. Dispatch actions and add payload if required.

2. Listen for changes in the store to know when a reducer finished its task.

An async load must not be split up. The calls are async, hence the state change may appear later, but nonetheless it lands in the component eventually.

Actions

Define the capabilities of your app, along with some default or initial value. In this example, Symbol defines the unique constants that are being used for any further request of an action:

```
export const INC = Symbol('INC');
export const DEC = Symbol('DEC');
export const SET = Symbol('SET');

export default {
  // initial value of payload,
  // this can be omitted if you don't care
  [INC]: () => 1,
```

```
  [DEC]: () => -1,
  SET
};
```

Figure A-7 shows the relevant parts of the action definition.

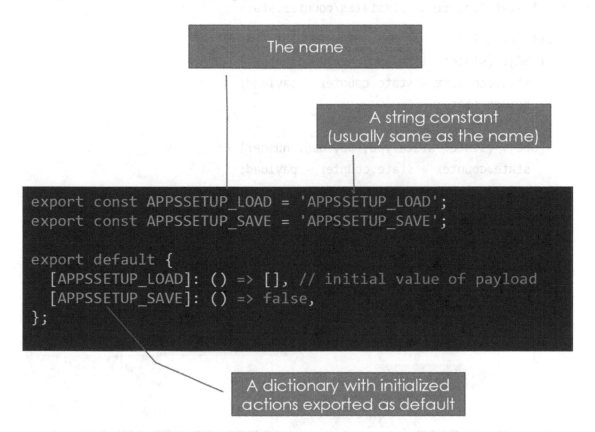

Figure A-7. *The main parts store: the action setup*

Why use actions?   It's convenient to have typed constants in the editor and to use easy-to-remember names without the chance to create mistakes.

Reducer

Define what happens if an action is dispatched:

```
import { INC, DEC } from '../actions/counter.action';
import stateType from '../states/counter.state';

export default {
    [INC]: (state: stateType, payload: number) => {
      state.counter = state.counter + payload;
      return state;
    },
    [DEC]: (state: stateType, payload: number) => {
      state.counter = state.counter - payload;
      return state;
    }
};
```

Figure A-8 shows the relevant parts of the reducer definition.

Reducer

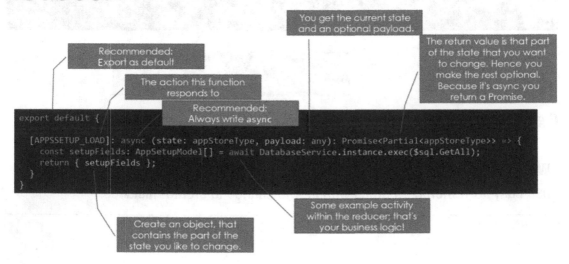

Figure A-8. *Parts of a reducer*

The returned payload is the whole store object by reference. The type for the store is optional and helps elevate the power of TypeScript and get a type-safe store.

Why use reducers at all?   Pure function calls are the foundation of a side-effect–free business layer. You have exactly one location where the logic goes: the reducer. That said, from now on you will know where to have logic, where to have UI, and where to store everything.

Reducers can be sync or async. Every function can be made as you like.

Return Value Considerations

The return value is an object that contains the fragments of the store that needs to be changed. Through subscriptions this is the way to inform other instances that something happened. But be careful with setting multiple values in one single step. The store logic will execute property by property and immediately publish the change event. A subscriber will receive the changes in the exact order of the properties in the reducer's returns value. If the subscriber receives the first property's change event, the new value is provided. However, the remaining values are not yet set, and hence the store is in an intermediate state. You must wait for all subscribers to get their final values. The best way to avoid hassle here is to avoid returning multiple values from a single reducer function.

Store and Dispatcher

The store holds the state, provides a dispatch function, and fires events in case a store value changes. First, the store can be defined by types, but this is an option and you may decide to go with a simple object just for the sake of simplicity. See Figure A-9.

```
import { StoreParams } from "@nyaf/store";

import { SomeModel } from "../model/some.model";

import theReducer from '../reducer/officematerial.reducer';
import theActions from '../actions/officematerial.actions';
import store from "app/services/flux/stores/global.store";

export interface SomeLocalStore {
    current: SomeModel;
    search: string;
}

export type someLocalStoreType = SomeLocalStore;

const initialStates: someLocalStoreType  = {
    current: null,
    search: ''
};

const theLocalStore: StoreParams<someLocalStoreType> = {
    actions: theActions,
    reducer: theReducer,
    state: initialStates
}

const mergedStore = store.mergeStore<someLocalStoreType>(theLocalStore);

export default mergedStore;
```

Import actions and reducers

Import the global store (optional, only if needed)

Define the store

Create a type for easier definitions

Define the initial state

Create the actual store object with actions and reducers and initial state

Merge the local store with the global one and return as default

15.06.2020

Figure A-9. *The store's parts*

The example shows a store that consists of fragments. This allows you to use parts of the store just by using the type fragments:

```
// This is a store fragment
export interface DemoTitleStore {
  title: string;
}
// This is a store fragment
export interface CounterStore {
  counter: number;
}
// This is the complete store, which can be used complete or in fragments
type store = CounterStore & DemoTitleStore;
// This is for convenient access
export default store;
```

Now see the usage within a component. First, you must configure the store with the elements written before. As shown, it's easy to combine reducers and add the various actions. To have the state typed, a generic is used.

```
import counterReducer from '../reducer/counter.reducer';
import setReducer from '../reducer/set.reducer';
import counterActions from '../actions/counter.action';
import storeStateType from '../states/counter.state';

const store = new Store<storeStateType>({
  actions: counterActions,
  mutations: { ...counterReducer, ...setReducer  },
  state: { counter: 0 }
});
```

Using the Store

Now make the store constant available in the component, if it's not yet defined there.
This store can handle just one single component or spread multiple components and
form eventually a single source of truth for the whole application.

```
@CustomElement('app-store-counter')
@ProvideStore<storeStateType>(store)
export class StoreCounterComponent
        extends BaseComponent<{ cnt: number }>
        implements IStore<storeStateType> {

  constructor() {
    super();
    this.setData('cnt', 0);
    // fire if a value changes in the store,
    // takes name of the store value
    this.store.subscribe('counter', str => {
      // write to a observed property to force re-render
      this.data.cnt = str.counter;
    });
  }

  clickMeAdd(e) {
    console.log('Counter Element Click INC');
    this.store.dispatch(INC, 1);
  }
```

```
clickMeSub(e) {
  console.log('Counter Element Click DEC');
  this.store.dispatch(DEC, 1);
}

clickMeSet(e) {
  console.log('Counter Element Click SET');
  this.store.dispatch(SET, 100);
}

render() {
  return (

    <div>
      <button type='button' n-on-click={this.clickMeAdd}>
        Add 1
      </button>
      <button type='button' n-on-click={this.clickMeSub}>
        Sub 1
      </button>
      <button type='button' n-on-click={this.clickMeSet}>
        Set 100
      </button>
    </div>
    <pre style='border: 1px solid gray;'>{this.data.cnt}</pre>

  );
 }
}
```

Pro Tip!   Combine this example with the forms module (@nyaf/forms) and get binding on the element level using the n-bind template feature.

Type Handling in Typescript

The store has these basic parts, as described before:

- Actions

- Reducer

- Store and store types

The actions are basically string constants. The reducers get the payload that's everything. The return value is the store type.

The store has two basic functions:

- dispatch

- subscribe

You dispatch an action along with a payload. So, the types are string and any.

When you receive a store event from a subscriber, this subscription watches for changes of a part of the store type. The event handler receives the whole store, then.

Example

Assume you are dealing with a CRUD (Create, Read, Update, Delete) component using a custom model like this:

```
import { Display } from '@nyaf/forms';
import { TemplateHint } from '@nyaf/forms';
import { Sortable } from '@nyaf/forms';
import { Hidden } from '@nyaf/forms';

export class ArchiveModel {
  @Hidden()
  id: number = 0;

  @Display('Closet')
  @Sortable()
  @TemplateHint('table-column', { width: 50 })
  Closet: string = '';
```

```
  @Display('Name')
  @Sortable()
  @TemplateHint('table-column', { width: 100 })
  Name: string = '';

  @Display('Surname')
  @Sortable()
  @TemplateHint('table-column', { width: 100 })
  Surname: string = '';

  @Display('Birthday')
  @TemplateHint('table-column', { width: 100 })
  Birthday: string = '';

  @Display('Number of Files')
  @TemplateHint('table-column', { width: 30 })
  NoFiles: number = 1;

  @Display('Archived')
  @Sortable()
  @TemplateHint('table-column', { width: 50 })
  ArchivedYear: number = 2010;
}
```

The decorators are from the _@nyaf/forms_ project.

Now, some actions are required:

```
import { ArchiveModel } from '../model/archiv.model';

export const ALL = 'ALL';
export const EDIT = 'EDIT';
export const ADD = 'ADD';
export const SAVE = 'SAVE';
export const REMOVE = 'REMOVE';

/**
 * The defaults that we use as long as the code hasn't sent anything.
 */
```

```
export default {
  [ALL]: () => '',
  [EDIT]: () => new ArchiveModel(),
  [ADD]: () => new ArchiveModel(),
  [SAVE]: () => new ArchiveModel(),
  [REMOVE]: () => 0,
};
```

Also, some reducers for doing the hard work:

```
import { ALL, ADD, REMOVE, EDIT, SAVE } from '../actions/archive.actions';
import { archiveStoreType } from '../stores/archive.store';
import { DatabaseService } from 'app/services/database.service';
import { DataGridModel } from 'app/components/shared/grid/models/datagrid.
model';
import { ArchiveModel } from '../model/archiv.model';

import * as $sql from 'app/resources/sql.json';

/**
 * The reducer functions are the executing logic. They "do" what the action
   is asking for.
 */
export default {
  [ALL]: async (state: archiveStoreType, payload: string) => {
    const data: any = await DatabaseService.instance.instance.exec($sql.
    ArchivAnzeigen);
    const modelData = new DataGridModel<ArchiveModel>(data, ArchiveModel);
    state.gridResult = modelData;
    return state;
  },
  [EDIT]: async (state: archiveStoreType, payload: number) => {
    const [current]: any = await DatabaseService.instance.instance.
    exec($sql.ArchivAnzeigenAktuelles, payload);
    state.current = current;
    return state;
  },
```

```
[ADD]: (state: archiveStoreType, payload: ArchiveModel) => {
  state.current = null;
  return state;
},
[SAVE]: async (state: archiveStoreType, payload: ArchiveModel) => {
  const data: any = await DatabaseService.instance.instance.exec(
    payload.id ? $sql.ArchiveUpdate : $sql.ArchiveInsert,
    payload.Closet,
    payload.Name,
    payload.Surname,
    payload.BirthDate,
    payload.NoFiles,
    payload.ArchivedYear,
    payload.id
  );
  const modelData = new DataGridModel<ArchiveModel>(data, ArchiveModel);
  state.gridResult = modelData;
  return state;
},
[REMOVE]: async (state: archiveStoreType, payload: number) => {
  const data: any = await DatabaseService.instance.instance.exec($sql.
  ArchiveRemoveFinal, payload);
  const modelData = new DataGridModel<ArchiveModel>(data, ArchiveModel);
  state.gridResult = modelData;
  return state;
},
};
```

DatabaseService.instance.instance is a service class with a singleton pattern. It executes SQL. $sql provides the statements from a resource file.

The store summarizes all this for easy processing:

```
import { ArchiveModel } from '../model/archiv.model';
import { DataGridModel } from 'app/components/shared/grid/models/datagrid.
model';
```

```
export interface ArchiveStore {
  current: ArchiveModel;
  gridResult: DataGridModel<ArchiveModel>;
}

/**
 * A store contains a data structure that holds up to the entire app's
   state.
 * It can have any complexity, from a single value up to deep nested
   objects.
 */
export interface ActionStore {
  search: string;
}

/**
 * We export a single store type that contains all single stores as one
   default.
 */
export type archiveStoreType = ActionStore & ArchiveStore;

import archiveReducer from '../reducer/archive.reducer';
import archiveActions, { SEARCH, ADD, REMOVE, ALL, ARCHIVED, EDIT } from
'../actions/archive.actions';
import { Store } from '@nyaf/store';

const store = new Store<archiveStoreType>({
  actions: archiveActions,
  reducer: { ...archiveReducer },
  state: { search: '', current: null, gridResult: null },
});

export default store;
```

Now, the component can dispatch actions with payloads and receive store changes:

```
@CustomElement('tab-archive-search')
@ProvideStore<archiveStoreType>(store)
```

```
export class ArchiveSearchComponent extends StoreComponent<archiveStoreTy
pe, {}> {
  constructor() {
    super();
    this.store.subscribe('gridResult', (data: archiveStoreType) => {
      // Do something with the data
    });
  }

  private async showAll(e?: Event) {
    this.store.dispatch(ALL, null);
  }

  // render omitted for brevity
}
```

The reducer receives the ALL action. It pulls all the data and sets the `gridResult` object. The subscriber listens for this and can handle the data (rerender, for example).

The essential part is here that the return value of the subscriber is always the Store Type (here `archiveStoreType`). So you don't need to think about the current type, and TypeScript resolves the types within properly. However, the subscriber is for just one property of the store and only changes of this property will trigger the handler. To get the data, access it like this:

```
archiveStoreType.gridResult;
```

The underlying object is `Proxy`, not your actual type.

Global and Local Stores

Technically there is just one store. But logically you will usually split the access into a global store (per app or module) and a local one (per component). See Figure A-10.

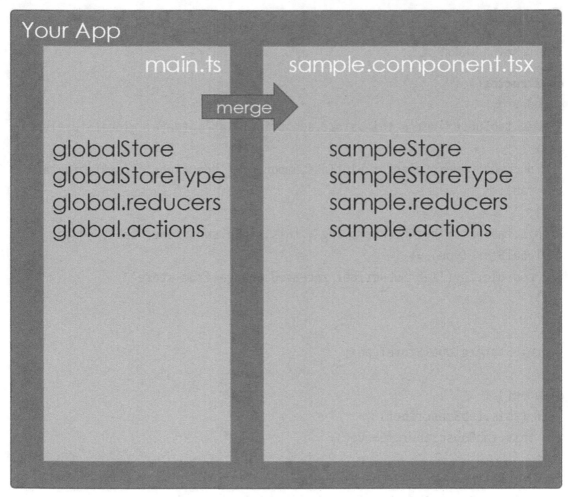

Figure A-10. *Global and local stores*

Merge Strategy

Within a component the stores are merged and appear as one unit afterwards.

Disposing

Some event handlers and especially the store environment need a proper removal of handlers. This happens in the `dispose` method you can override in the component.

Example

This is how it looks:

```
constructor() {
  super();
  this.tabSubscriber = this.store.subscribe('tab', (data: globalStoreType)
  => {
    document.querySelector<SlotTabsComponent>('#dcmoTabs')?.setTab(data.
    tab);
  });
  this.tabSubscriberCheckRemoving = this.store.subscribe('tab', (data:
  globalStoreType) => {
    console.log('Tab Subscriber received change from store');
  });
}

store: Store<globalStoreType>;

dispose() {
  if (this.tabSubscriber) {
    this.tabSubscriber.remove();
  }
  if (this.tabSubscriberCheckRemoving) {
    this.tabSubscriberCheckRemoving.remove();
  }
}
```

Even easier is the usage of the Dispose decorator:

```
@Dispose(s => s.remove()) private readonly tabSubscriber;
@Dispose(s => s.remove()) private readonly tabSubscriberCheckRemoving;
```

You can now remove the dispose method entirely.

General Usage

The @Dispose decorator is defined in the base library and not limited to store actions.

Effects Mapping

A component is basically just a UI that is defined by HTML. This UI can be dynamic in both directions, receiving user actions and reacting to changes in an underlying data model. In business components, this leads to a significant amount of code that is primarily just a reference to the coding environment. For user actions, it's a number of event hooks leading to handlers. For data changes, it's the binding to a model and code to monitor changes.

The Flux store reduces the amount of code by moving the actual business logic to the reducer functions. This is a big process compared to traditional programming styles, but the remaining definitions are now only skeletons to function calls. It would be great to have these function calls reduced to the bare minimum of code and, in the same step, collected in one single definition just like the reducers. This feature exists in @nyaf and it's called *effects*.

The Effects Decorator

The decorator exists once on a component. The API looks like this:

```
@Effects(Effect[])
```

It makes sense only in conjunction with the store itself. This is how it goes with a real component:

```
@CustomElement('app-store-effects')
@ProvideStore<allStoreTypes>(store)
@Effects([
  {
    selector: 'button[data-action="ADD"]',
    trigger: 'click',
    parameter: (e) => (e.target as HTMLElement).dataset.payload || 1,
    action: INC
  }
])
export class StoreEffectsComponent extends BaseComponent<{ cnt: number }>
implements IStore<allStoreTypes> {
}
```

Imagine this code in a component without effects:

```
<button class='btn btn-md btn-success' type='button' n-on-click={e => this.
clickMeAdd(e)}>
  Add 1
</button>

clickMeAdd(e) {
  this.store.dispatch(INC, 1);
}
```

The whole purpose of the code is to add a click event and trigger the dispatcher.
Effects move both parts outside of the component and you can remove the code entirely.
The view becomes simpler and the component is smaller and less error-prone.

Using the Effects Decorator

To keep the handler stuff outside the component and still connected to one, you use a
decorator. The following example gives you an impression how it could look:

```
@Effects([
{
  selector: '[data-action="ADD"]',
  trigger: 'click',
  parameter: (e) => (e.target as HTMLElement).dataset.payload || 1,
  action: INC
},
{
  selector: '[data-action="SUB"]',
  trigger: 'click',
  parameter: (e) => (e.target as HTMLElement).dataset.payload || 1,
  action: DEC
},
{
  selector: '[data-action="SET"]',
  trigger: 'click',
  parameter: (e) => +(e.target as HTMLElement).dataset.payload,
```

```
  action: SET
}
])
```

The decorator accepts an array of objects of type Effect. This type is an interface that has the following API:

- selector: A string that can be handled by querySelectorAll
- trigger: A string that is one of the common ECMAScript events an element can fire or any custom event name
- action: A string constant that the store's reducer accepts in a dispatch call
- parameter: An (optional) function that retrieves a value from the event handler parameter

The Selector

The selector is a string that can be handled by querySelectorAll. This is mandatory and the selector must return at least one element. The selector is executed after the life cycle event state Load. This means that the render function is executed. The selector will not get any elements you add later dynamically.

To avoid any conflicts, it's strongly recommended to use data- attributes and avoid any CSS stuff to select elements, especially the class attribute.

The Trigger

The trigger is a string that is one of the common ECMAScript events an element can fire or any custom event name. To support IntelliSense, a number of common events are part of the definition, but technically it's allowed to use any string here. Internally the event is attached to the outcome of the selector by using addEventHandler(trigger).

The Action Definition

The action is a string constant that the store's reducer accepts in a dispatch call. It's recommended to use the action constants and not provide any string values here directly. The binder class that handles this internally will throw an exception if the action is not known by the store.

The Parameter

The parameter is a function that retrieves a value from the event handler parameter. This is the only optional value. You can omit it if the dispatched action does not need a payload. For all other reducer calls, this function returns a value that is used as the payload.

The returned type is always any without further restrictions.

The input parameter is the event's parameter object. In most cases, it's of type Event, KeyEvent, or MouseEvent. In case of a custom component it could be CustomEvent. To retrieve values, the best way is to access the source element by using this code snippet:

```
const element = (e.target as HTMLElement);
```

To provide dynamic values, the data- attributes are a robust way of doing so. To access the values directly, use the dataset property. If your attribute is further divided in sections using the kebab-style (such as in data-action-value) the dataset property converts this into camel case (action-value transforms into actionValue). But you can use any other property of the event source to set values. You can also simply use static values, too. However, even if technically possible, it's not recommended to add any business logic or validation code in these functions. Move such code consequently to the reducer. Otherwise your logic code will be split up and will become very hard to maintain. The reason the @Effects decorator exists is just to get a more rigid structure in your app.

Automatic Updates

The @Updates decorator complements the @Effects decorator. The schema is similar. However, both decorators work independently of each other and you can use either or both.

The Updates Decorator

The decorator exists once on a component. The API looks like this:

```
@Updates(Update[])
```

It only makes sense in conjunction with the store itself (a missing store will throw an exception). This is how it goes with a real component:

```
@CustomElement('app-store-effects')
@ProvideStore<allStoreTypes>(store)
@Updates<allStoreTypes>([
  {
    store: 'counter',
    selector: '[data-store-counter]',
    target: 'textContent'
  }
])
export class StoreUpdateComponent extends BaseComponent<{ cnt: number }>
implements IStore<allStoreTypes> {
}
```

The piece of HTML that this @Update decorator setting addresses is shown below:

```
<div class='badge badge-info' data-store-counter>n/a</div>
```

There is no additional code required to update the HTML. Once a change in the store occurs, the value is pulled from the store and written into the selected property. In the example, the store's value 'counter' is monitored by a subscription. The elements are selected once in the lifecycle state Load. Further changes of the component's DOM are not processed. The access works with or without a Shadow DOM. The element's selector in the example is '[data-store-counter]'. You can use any selector querySelectorAll would accept. If there are multiple elements indeed, the assignment will happen multiple times. The target property is textContent. You can use any property that the selected element or component supports. Be aware that the access is property access on the code level. That means a virtual attribute of a component will not work because it's not changed in the markup. If you have a component as the target and wish to write a value to an observed attribute, you must introduce getter and setter methods to support the @Update decorator.

In the example, the store definition (using @ProvideStore) and the update configuration (using @Updates) use the very same store type. This is not necessary. If the store type is a combined type (as in the example code you can find on GitHub), consider using one of its partial types for the update to shrink the selection to the part you really need. This avoids errors and improves the readability of your code.

Using the Updates Decorator

The following code shows the typical store subscription, usually assigned in the constructor:

```
this.sub = this.store.subscribe('counter', str => {
  this.querySelector('[data-store-counter]').textContent = str.counter;
});
```

The value is written in a freshly selected element. The very same result can be achieved with the following code:

```
@Updates<allStoreTypes>([ {
    store: 'counter',
    selector: '[data-store-counter]',
    target: 'textContent'
}])
```

While this does not seem to be a big advantage (in fact, it is two lines more), the real reason is to avoid **any** code in the component directly, making it pure view. In the long term, this creates clean code and helps to make a more systematic structure.

The decorator accepts an array of objects of type `Update`. This type is an interface that has the following API:

- `selector`: A string that can be handled by `querySelectorAll`.

- `store`: A string that is one of the properties of the store type. This is managed by the generic.

- `target`: A string that's the name of a property the selected element or component supports. This is not checked by TypeScript.

The Selector

The selector is a string that can be handled by `querySelectorAll`. This is mandatory and the selector must return at least one element. The selector is executed after the life cycle event state `Load`. This means that the `render` function is executed. The selector will not get any elements you add later dynamically.

To avoid any conflicts, it's strongly recommended to use `data-` attributes and avoid any CSS stuff to select elements, especially not the `class` attribute.

The Store

The store usually has a type definition to define the fundamental structure. Usually it's just an interface. The generic provides this type definition and you can choose any of these properties. Internally it's a keyof T definition.

The Target

Because you can't write a value straight into an element or into a component you must define a specific property. The type is either any of the properties supported by HTMLElement or just a string. This is weak from the standpoint of IntelliSense (in fact, there is actually no check at all), but flexible enough to support all common scenarios.

It's a tradeoff between convenience and security. A more rigid approach would require a generic on the level of the Update interface. But with an anonymous type definition you can't provide a generic. This means you need to add additional type information. In the end, it's a lot more boilerplate code for a little safety. This is why the definition can be made so simple.

Installation

Install the store package like this:

```
npm i @nyaf/store -S
```

The type definitions required for TypeScript are part of the packages and no additional type libraries are required.

Dependencies

The one and only dependency is the core library, @nyaf/lib.

Summary

This appendix is the complete documentation of my Web Components library @ nyaf. I wrote this library in the context of several customer projects while using Web Components in real-life projects. It turns out that Web Components are both amazingly powerful and surprisingly weak. There are good reasons for frameworks such as React, Vue, and Angular. However, the significant shrink of bundle sizes, the amazing speed of native code, the low usage of memory, and the ability to use the full power of HTML 5 APIs are big advantages. It's a tradeoff. Finally, I found that state, validation, and routing are features we can't rule out. You will need those things, eventually. This was the point when I started to implement one or the other piece of code to avoid coding repeating tasks (remember the DRY principle).

After a while, the skeleton of this library became visible. I coded all the parts down to whatever was necessary for typical projects, just to see the size of the outcome. If it was exactly the same size as the frameworks mentioned, there would be no benefit. I was surprised that the basic version was just a few KB of code. Of course, some error handling could be better and often the error messages are, yes, no error messages at all. But it's feature-complete, fast, and powerful. It's the power of Web Components and HTML 5 that unleashes this power, along with the avoidance of any look back. This means no support for older browsers.

Have a look at `http://nyaf.comzept.de/` to get the latest documentation. Follow the instruction to pull the package from npm and get the sources from GitHub. And, last but not least, any feedback is highly appreciated.

Index

Printed in the United States
by Baker & Taylor Publisher Services